RUSSELL GRANT'S

1994 HOROSCOPES

CAPRICORN

22 December-20 January

First published in Great Britain in 1993 by
Virgin Books
an imprint of Virgin Publishing Ltd
332 Ladbroke Grove
London W10 5AH

Illustrations by Maggie Kneen

A catalogue record for this title is available from the British
Library

ISBN 0 86369 659 7

Typeset by Phoenix Photosetting, Chatham, Kent.
Printed in Great Britain by
Cox & Wyman Ltd, Reading, Berks.

CONTENTS

INTRODUCTION

Welcome to the latest edition of my astrological almanac, full of information about the starry trends coming your way in nectarine 1994!

If you've been wondering what the New Year has in store for you, then you need look no further than the packed pages of this book, for it contains all you need to know for an enjoyable, enterprising and successful annum. If you're a regular reader of my columns and books, then you'll know by now that astrology is all about forecasting the possible pitfalls, problems and potentials indicated by the planets' positions and relationships in the heavens. It can't determine your destiny, because only you can do that by exercising your free will, but what it can do is point out all the good and bad vibes that are surrounding you. Then you can cash in on every opportunity that comes your way, or turn nasty or negative situations to your advantage by being prepared for them in advance. And there's a special section outlining your amorous, pecuniary and professional prospects over the coming year. Let's face it, we can all be wise after the event, but wouldn't it be better to be wise beforehand?

Do you ever feel that you hold yourself back from making the most of your life, are full of fears and phobias or dogged by depression, doom and despondency? If so, it seems that stringent and serious Saturn occupies a powerful position in your birthchart, so turn to my special section on this perplexing planet to discover more about the inner you and how to make Saturn work for you, not against you.

Want to make the most of the coming year and turn it into a treasure trove of good fortune, potential and enjoyment? Then plot generous Jupiter's path through your horoscope with my simple chart, and let this prosperous planet be your guide to a bumper 1994!

Wondering why a relationship's reached rock bottom, or want to know how you'll fare with someone you've just met? Then look no further than my chapters on the twelve Sun signs, and also my relationship guide, to learn everything you need to know about getting on with others. Want to know your lucky number, day of the week or birthstone? Then turn to my chart giving the traditions of astrology, and start reading!

Ever wondered which famous folk share your Sun sign, or even your birthday? Then have a look at my special guide to the star dates of the stars – you may even discover an astrological twin or two!

Once you've read all that, plus my day-by-day forecasts, you'll be all set for a propitious, providential and positive new year. Enjoy yourself!

RUSSELL'S GUIDE TO THE SUN SIGNS

ARIES – 21 MARCH–20 APRIL

Me, me, me, me! No, it's not an opera singer practising the scales, but the Arien catch-phrase. This is the first sign of the zodiac, and Ariens like everyone to remember that. (First come, first served, is the Martian motto.) And because this is such a fun-loving, frisky sign, Ariens can get away with it.

The positive side of Aries is like a scene from *The African Queen*, in which our intrepid explorers boldly go where only crocodiles have gone before. Ariens are active, alive, awake (usually), assertive and adventurous, hacking their way through the undergrowth of life like Marlon Brando in a steamy movie. (Yes, he's an Arien!) But they can take this exuberance to extremes. (They can take a lot of things to extremes!) Ariens can step out, putting their best feet forward (all four of them – well,

3

they are animals!) and sinking up to their best end of necks in trouble.

Luscious Libra is the polar sign of assertive Aries, and these signs have a lot to learn from each other. Librans always put others first, which is something Ariens find almost impossible to do. In fact, a relationship between these two is their idea of heaven, because they both think about the Arien. (And of course, after 'Me', the Ram's favourite word is 'Ewe'!)

Sometimes, this can cause a contretemps in the course of true love. Male Ariens may forget about the wife and six kids at home and gad about like a bachelor gay with a collection of conquests. Arien women may throw their weight about too, demanding new dresses and wanting to be taken to the best restaurants, even when their men haven't got two halfpennies to rub together.

Aries is ruled by Mars, the planet that gives them that gorgeous get-up-and-go, that delicious drive and determination. (As long as they're not determinedly driving all over delicious *you*!) Mighty Mars rules Scorpio, too, when he shares the limelight with powerful Pluto. Then he can make Scorpios furtive and underhand, but when he's in open Aries, it's a very different story. Ariens can be so candid and frank that it's an excruciating experience to hear them. You can meet your Martian mate for a meal, and swan in, looking sensational. (Or so you think, you poor dear.) The Arien will take one look at you and say 'That frock makes you look fatter than ever.' (How can you then say that you've just lost two stone – and a pal in the process!)

There's something rather ingenuous about Aries. Because this is the first sign of the zodiac, Rams represent the babies of the celestial sky. Sometimes they're so naive and innocent it's astounding, and they'll dash off and do or say something really reckless. (Or just plain potty!) They can also have terrible temper tantrums, like a tirading toddler, and shout and scream till they're blue in the face.

Assertive Ariens are so determined to get what they want that they'll let nothing stand in their way. They'll go on until it kills them.

Every sign has its own song, and the Arien's aria must be 'Let's Get Physical'. (Take that in any way you like. After all, they will!) Rams are imbued with enough physical energy to fill a whole football team (and a stand of supporters!). But, like children, they have to find positive pursuits in which to burn it all off. Ariens are full of fire, fun, vivacity, verve and virility. (Quite a captivating concoction, which can really go to your head!) But they can fritter away their fantastic physical fitness, and instead of having an active social, sports or sex life, turn to violence and vandalism. (Even the meekest and mildest mutton will show a strong side sometimes, and may bop you on the bonce for no apparent reason.) Some of these Martians can be all brawn and no brain, thinking with their fists – or any other part of the anatomy that springs to mind! (Ariens have powerful passions and strong sex drives!)

Ariens are like medieval knights, arrayed in armour and jousting for superiority. Their Fiery natures make them compulsively competitive, and determined to do battle. They have *got* to come first. Rams, lambs and sheep hate losing, whether at Ludo, life or love. (They'll just throw the dice for a six and start again.) When they see success slipping away, they'll fight tooth and claw, frightening off folk in their flocks. Watch out, watch out, there's a Ram about!

TAURUS – 21 APRIL–21 MAY

Taureans are very easy creatures to understand. They have very basic needs: male Bulls love grub and girls, and females of this sign adore food and fellas. Simple, isn't it?

Being the first of the Earth signs, Taurus symbolises rich,

rolling fields of very dark brown earth waiting to be culti-
vated. The Sun sits in the sign of Taurus at Maytime, and so
Taurus is linked with the ritual of May Day, the maypole,
young maidens, and earthy, pagan customs and folklore.

Taureans are governed by their love of sensuality in all its
forms, and some of them can go a mite mad and overindulge themselves, whether it's with sex or a simmering stew
with delicious dumplings.

A lot of Taureans have very expressive, often deep-set
eyes, that can put across their message better than a million
Gemini words. I know one normally sensible, sane
Capricorn girl who was reduced to a gibbering wreck when
one of these Bulls looked at her across a crowded room. He
didn't have to say a word – his eyes did all the talking. (I'd
wondered why she suddenly blushed like a beetroot.)

Bulls hate change. They need to know that tomorrow
will be the same as today, and that the day after tomorrow
will be the same as a week next Wednesday. This is not a
sign that is moved by facing a challenge, but Bulls can show
tremendous endeavour, patience, persistence and
resoluteness.

I have many Taurean chums, and what I absolutely adore
about them is that when you go to visit them, you will have
barely opened the garden gate before they've offered you a
cuppa and asked you if you've eaten. (Say no.) They can be
wonderfully warm and welcoming, really making you feel
at home, and wondering what they can give you that is
theirs. (More stew?)

Ownership is very important to Taureans. Seeing a room
full of furniture they've paid for, or a freezer full of food,
makes them feel secure. However, negative Taureans can
be so possessive and narrow-minded that they can class
wives, husbands, kids and pets in the same category as the
couch and the cooker and feel that they own them lock,
stock and barrel.

To give you an idea of the good and bad sides of the Bull,

a country said to be ruled by Taurus is the Emerald Isle. Think of the simple, relaxed way of life there, those glorious greens and beautiful browns of the Irish countryside; then think of the widespread bigotry over religion with both sides refusing to compromise, and you have Taurus at its worst.

In fact, one description of Taurus that you will hear time and time again is 'stubborn as a mule'. Certainly, Taurus is a Fixed sign, and Taureans can be as hard to shift as a sack of soggy cement, but I do think this so-called stubbornness is a wee bit overemphasised. Of course, there is a diabolical dose of dogged determination in the Taurean character, but these Bulls are not always as obstinate and obtuse as they are portrayed. In fact, if used positively, this steadfast streak can lead to persistence and determination. On the negative side, it can lead to rumbustious rows because of the Taurean's intransigence and inability to see another person's point of view.

But make no mistake. If used in the right way, fixity can be a wonderful thing. If Bulls want something slightly out of reach, they will put their heads down and charge (slowly) straight for it, eventually achieving their goal, even if it kills them in the process!

As you might expect from a sign that symbolises the countryside, often Taureans aren't very happy in the city – unlike Air or Fire signs, who like hustle and bustle. Taureans, on the other hand, need to live in a place where they can commune with nature, feeling the ground beneath their feet and seeing the sky above their heads. Bulls will be at their best in a verdant village, or a comfy crofter's cottage. City Bulls will have stacks of window boxes crammed with leafy flora, to give them that 'at home' feeling. Bulls' abodes will be warm and welcoming, unless they are going through a desperate disruption or change in their relationships.

Taureans rarely do anything quickly, choosing to take

their time. If they're negative, they may prefer to pretend that their position, passionwise, is pootchy, when even the fly on the wall can see that it isn't. Eventually the world will crumble around their ears, when their amour ambles off with another. Everyone except the Bull will have seen exactly what was happening, and not be outraged at the outcome.

Taureans find it especially difficult to accept change in their emotional relationships, because fidelity and loyalty are paramount to them. But whether a Taurean likes it or not (probably not), changes of some sort or another will be inevitable in their lives, and the sooner they get used to the idea the better. The more they can make themselves cope with change, the less heartache they will have in the long run. I know many Taureans who have resisted an upheaval that was inevitable, and gone through hell and high water as a result.

Venus rules Taurus and Libra, endowing both signs with a love of beauty and a need for harmony, although they seek these ideals in different ways. When ruling Libra, Venus is lighter and more sanguine, but she's much deeper and richer in Taurus. Librans love Rodgers and Hammerstein, while Taureans will opt for opera. They love the beauty of flowers, the earth and all the good things in life, and with their classical, traditional outlook, can teach a lot of the more restless signs quite a lesson or two. So don't fall into the trap of thinking Taureans are simply bull-headed. They can be obstinate, though they would call it being strong-minded!

GEMINI – 22 MAY–21 JUNE

If you want to know how a Gemini ticks, sidle up to the one you're trying to puzzle out, start up a chatette, and then listen very carefully. Above the twinkling tones of the Twin twittering on, you may hear a weird whirring, combined with a couple of clicks. Yes? Well, congratulations, my dears, you have just heard the Gemini brain cells in action. And they are what make every Gemini tick.

The more astute Twins will actually admit to being aware of their Mercurial minds working. They can *feel* themselves thinking. Just imagine all those neurons neoning away inside their noddles. Geminis think so quickly that they leave some of the other signs standing. Everything they see and hear will pass through that brilliant brainbox and be stored away for future reference in the Geminian filing system.

If you're meeting a Gemini for the first time, you'll notice how nervously and quickly he or she moves. Even if the Twin is sitting talking to you, his or her eyes will be taking in everything in the room, and everything about you. Even the egg stain on your tie and the fascinating fact that you're wearing odd socks!

Geminis have a very low boredom threshold, and you'll soon know if you've made them cross it. Their peepers will be poring all over the place and rarely popping back to you. (Apart from your egg stain, of course, because they'll be dying to ask you if it was boiled or fried.) Their fingers will begin to tap out tunes on the table, their feet will jiggle up and down, and they will become fantastically fidgety. This is a danger sign, and unless you can suddenly turn the conversation on to a different, more scintillating subject, to ignite their interest again, you may as well give up and go home. Otherwise you'll be written off as being too boring to bother with.

All Geminis have an elfin appearance, and look like potential pixies. It's rare for them to look like hobgoblins, because this is a very attractive sign, both mentally and physically. The typical Twin – male or female – is incredibly pretty in a boyish way, with alert, shining eyes and fine features.

Most Twins have a very fast way of talking, and may even start to stammer when excited. That may sound strange when you consider that Geminis are so glib and garrulous, and graced with the gift of the gab, but actually sometimes their minds move faster than their mouths, and you get a right old scramble coming out! Geminis love puns because it means they can play about with their favourite toys – words.

Every sign has its good and bad side, and Gemini is no exception. Positively, Geminis are incredibly lively, witty people, extremely articulate and natural communicators. But the reverse of that is the Twin who uses communications in the wrong way, and tells terrible lies (like Matilda's, they make one gasp and stretch one's eyes). Some Geminis like to bend the truth into real reef knots: they can be real Uri Gellers with words.

A lot of Geminis say to me, 'Oh, I'm two-faced, because I'm a Twin,' but I think they've got it wrong. The popular myth is that all Geminis are raving schizophrenics, or Jekyll and Hyde characters, being sweet as sugar one minute and ravening beasties the next. You have to look at Gemini's ruling planet, Mercury, to work this out. As it spins about the solar system, one side of it is always in darkness, and the other is always light. And it's the same with the Twins. When we talk of dark and light in a personality, we can mean a true schizophrenic, with two personalities in one mind, or simply someone, like a Gemini, who experiences a tremendous variety of emotions within *one* personality. Geminis can certainly have extremes of character, and on one level be alert, bright, chatty and chirpy, and on another, be so depressed they can't even find the words to describe how miserable they are.

Very often, Geminis can be desperately disappointed with the world. It can be such a dull place, full of such dreary people that Twins have to invent their own, brighter world to cheer themselves up. Geminian memories of events are always a slightly different version of what really happened!

If you understand this it'll help you to appreciate the Twins you know better. You should even feel a bit sorry for them, if you think about it. People who live in their heads that much are bound to be lonely, at least some of the time.

CANCER – 22 JUNE–23 JULY

Cuddle and caress a Cancerian you know, today! Crabs need to feel safe and secure, and to know that they are adored and amoured.

This is the sign of Moons and Junes – literally! Leo is led by the Sun, but Cancer is ruled by the other leading light of the zodiac, the Moon. Throughout history and legend, the Moon has always represented motherhood, and she rules the tides, menstruation, and everything else associated with the 28-day cycle. (No, it's not a new form of transport!) The Moon is the peaceful, passive, defensive drive within us, and in the natal chart she shows our maternal instincts, habits and childhoods, and whether we love or loathe our mums.

Generally speaking, Cancerians are ultra-protective, and that can mean they protect themselves as well as others. (Well, aren't crabs encased in shells?) A very good friend of mine says that if you think of a rocker, clad in chain mail and leather, looking fearfully ferocious, then try to imagine taking all that chain mail off, you'll find a very ordinary person underneath. And you can say exactly the same thing about Cancer the Crab. There they are, with that solid shell, that concrete coating, waving their pincers about provocatively, and pretending to be pugnacious. But get out the crab cracker and you have the main ingredient for a rather nice crab sandwich – sweet and soft! (Slap two slices of brown bread around them, quick!)

11

When you first meet a Cancerian, you will sense a hardness, tetchiness and moodiness, as Crabs are always on the defensive! These are the folk who rush into the room and slap you round the face, just in case you're going to be nasty!

On a positive level, this is a devoted sign. Crabs have a fierce family feeling, can get quite clannish, and put their kith and kin at the centre of their universes.

Many Cancerian men tie the nuptial knot, but can't untangle the apron strings that bind them to their mums and dads. This can cause fantastic flare-ups within their marriages, because their wives feel upstaged by their mothers-in-law. And lots of Cancerian women spend almost all their weekends with their parents in the bosom (what a nice Cancerian word!) of their families, even when they've got a husband and six kids at home. (Maybe that's why!)

Crabs can remember what they had for breakfast on their second birthdays, but they can also remember when you last let them down. They will hurl back past slights, which happened many moons before, in the middle of a row. They also like to live in the past (ever seen a Crab in a crinoline?), and they're very traditional, and tremendous collectors of bits and bobs, especially if they are full of memories. (They call them mementoes. Other people call them tat.) And they hoard letters like mad! (A true Crab will have kept all the letters he or she has ever received from the age of six months onwards.)

You see, they hate to throw things away. (Just in case they come in handy.) A Cancerian friend of mine once went whizzing off to a jumble sale at eleven in the morning loaded with the memorabilia (another good Cancerian word) she was chucking out. At half past three she bought the lot back for ten bob. She couldn't bear to part with a single sock!

Being a Water sign, and ruled by the Moon, Crabs are powerfully psychic, and they will have incredibly intuitive instincts. (When they say they're tuning in, they're not talking about the radio!) Crowds of Cancerians can walk into a room and instantly pick up an atmosphere. (And I don't mean the sultry scent of Saturday's supper – sprouts and stew – either.) Their superb sensitivity also means they can be hurt far too easily, and often over nothing at all. Some of them are hypersensitive, and should realise that when they are told something, it's not always meant as a criticism, or an out-and-out rejection.

Cancerians should try to toughen their soft skins which sit beneath their shells, and not harbour hurts or supposed slights. When they do take umbrage, they become changeable and crabby, mean, moody, huffy and hostile, and almost unapproachable at times. They should use their highly-developed instincts in a positive manner, and trust them and live by them. (Very intense Crabs will tune into their teapots, saying at about four in the afternoon, 'I feel I should put the kettle on.' If you're there, try saying you can sense a custard cream hovering in the biscuit tin.)

Security is of vital importance to Cancerians; often if they feel down and depressed, and are doddering about in the doldrums, it's because they don't have a real base to go home to. They need the emotional security of having their own four walls about them, whereas Taureans need nests for material security.

If you're married to a Cancerian, or have a chum who's a Crab, you have to behave like a cuckoo clock, and at every half hour pop your head round the door and say 'I love you!' (You must mean it, though.) Then they'll feel safe and secure. (Go on, give 'em a kiss!) They can be so gruff that they take you by surprise sometimes. So, if you know a Cancerian who is being crabby, just remember the rocker with the chain mail. (If you're a Bull, you'll remember the crab sandwich!) Underneath that hard shell shimmers a heart of pure gold, which is just waiting to melt as the first words of love cascade from your lips!

Now, of course, there are some cantankerous, cross and cranky Crabs about. They'll be mean and moody, and will scowl like scallops. They'll click away with their pincers, sounding like a couple of castanets on a package holiday, but they will still be soft and sweet underneath.

Cancerians really do need to be needed, and know that they're loved. Otherwise, they can't function fully. Remember this is the polar sign of Capricorn, and most Goats are frightened of rejection. Crabs can be just the same. If they do have particularly firm filial feelings, especially for a matriarchal mum, they'll prefer to hide at home than go out into the big wide world and face whatever it may have to offer them. And when they do scuttle out from under a rock to test the waters of life, if they're used and abused, they'll sound a furious fandango with their perpetually pirouetting pincers, and then rush back to the boulder as fast as their pins can propel them.

Babies are a must for this sign. Whereas procreation is important for Leos, who love children and like to be proud of their own cubs, with Cancer it is much deeper, and more a case of carrying on the family name. Cynthia Crab. Cyril Crab . . .

LEO – 24 JULY–23 AUGUST

Inside every Leo is a king or queen waiting to jump out. (In a little Leo it'll be a prince or princess.) But whatever the rank, Leos do like to wear the crown, hold the sceptre, and be in charge. It's a Leo who will lead a little old lady across the road, even when she doesn't want to go! (You try arguing with a Lion halfway across a zebra crossing!)

Leo's aren't going to like this, but what makes many of them tick is acres of applause. They like to be the centre of attention and know that their public – whether it's 5000 fans or the boy next door – appreciates them.

There are some very colourful Leos around, but there are some very grey ones too. Think of a Leo, and you'll see someone blond and blue-eyed, with a magnificent mane of hair. The men always look like Apollo, who is associated with this sunny sign. And the women are stunningly striking, and have long golden tresses (even if they are out of a bottle!), which shimmer every time they toss their heads in a majestic manner. However, there's another sort, too. This breed look a little like moles, not lions at all, with black barnets, piggy peepers and a rather shifty air! It's very hard to believe that they belong to this splendid sign, but they do!

But whatever they look like, there's no doubt that positive Leos will offer you the earth and give you their hearts. (Gold-plated ones, of course.) There is a gorgeous grandiosity about Leos, but sometimes they can be all mouth. It's only when it's too late that you realise the Lion was just out to impress you.

There was a Lion I used to know, who would offer everyone the earth. He made you feel there was nothing he wouldn't do for you, and promises, offers and assurances flew from his mouth like bees from a hive. The trouble was that those bees never made any honey! It was all hot air, and that's very disappointing indeed from a Lion.

You must never forget (as if the Lions would let you!) that Leo is ruled by the Sun, the centre of the solar system. This star controls almost everything and we'd die without the heat from its rays. So, a lot of Leos can live their lives with a Sun complex. The modest wee beasts feel that as the Sun is the centre of the solar system, so they are centre of the human race!

As a result, of course, they expect people to put down the red carpet for them. Everything has to be done in a stately, stylish way, as if entertaining royalty. When a Leo comes to tea, he or she won't want to be fobbed off with just one fairy cake, but will demand a three-tiered Victoria sponge. This is a regal, dignified and imperial sign, and the Leo will be either an Emperor Nero or Good Queen Bess. But whatever part he or she is playing, it has to be one that doesn't go unnoticed. Leos don't like to be just one of the crowd, like an extra in a scene from *Gone With the Wind*. They want to be Rhett Butler or Scarlett O'Hara. (Lions with strong Cancerian links will want to play Tara, the O'Hara home!)

In astrology, the Sun is our creative core, so Leo is said to be the most creative of the signs. Leos may portray this by playing Annie in *Annie Get Your Gun* at the local amateur dramatic society or by painting their self-portraits on a 40-foot canvas. If they can't be creative themselves in an active way, they'll do it passively, taking off to the theatre or burying themselves in a book. (Why not start with this one?)

Make no mistake, Leo is the sign of the Hollywood musical extravaganza. It may be a bit brash, but it'll have a massive orchestra, and you'll be spellbound by the majesty of it all. And that's what Leos love most. Neptune was tripping the light fantastic through Leo during the great age of Hollywood musicals, which is why they were so lavish. And believe it or not, lots of film producers and directors are Leos – Sam Goldwyn, Alfred Hitchcock, Busby Berkeley and Cecil B. DeMille were all born under this splendid sign of the silver screen. (Leos certainly know how to do things in style.)

There's a fantastic feeling of leisure and pleasure about this sign. Leos love enjoying themselves. (And that's not as obvious as it sounds. Virgos and Capricorns sometimes feel guilty when they have a good knees-up.) They also adore being seen with the right people. (Up-market Leos will be the people the other Leos want to be seen with!)

What makes most Leos tick, though, is very simple. It's the biggest heart imaginable – a sort of titanic ticker. Positive Lions can be wonderfully warm and lastingly loving. And as if that weren't enough, they have a rich sense of

16

humour running through them that will surround you and make you feel safe and secure.

Some Leos aren't lovable Lions at all, but are cheetahs, literally. This sneaky side of the sign comes from the Leonine lust for power. These crafty cats won't have the personality or warmth of the positive Leo, so will have to achieve their ambitions through underhand acts. Don't expect all Leos to want to be centre-stage, because some of them will prefer to wait in the wings, looking on. But most Leos love the limelight, and are happier playing the main man or leading lady. (They may even stick gold stars on their bedroom doors at home.) These Leos aren't concerned with the chorus; they want the bright lights and all that goes with them. Their love of luxury means they can look and dress the part to perfection. But very often they'll behave abominably, and treat everyone as if they were their servants. Don't let a Lion make you his or her skivvy!

Just because a Leo chooses *not* to come on like a Hollywood hotchpotch of Mae West, Cleopatra (don't let her get the needle) and Napoleon Bonaparte, doesn't mean he or she is negative. Sometimes, it's quite the reverse! All you need is a peek at a pirouetting and preening prima donna to see what produces a positive Leo. Some Lions will convey their creative concerto in a quieter, more controlled way. (A Moonlight Sonata rather than an 1812 Overture!) But a positive pussycat will always be the sunshine of your life.

VIRGO – 24 AUGUST–23 SEPTEMBER

Now, before we go any further, think about the Virgos you know. (They're the ones with the neat hairdos and shiny shoes, who make you feel as if you've just been dragged through a hedge backwards.) One of the wonderful things about Virgos is their tremendous talent for organising everything under the sun – starting with themselves. And they really come into their own when they can organise others as well, whether as a cleaning lady or as Home Secretary.

Vestal Virgos of all shapes and sizes are only too pleased to give you a helping hand; their Mercurial motto is 'Service with a smile'. What's more, they really live up to it. You can phone your friend when you're in a fix, and the Virgo will zoom round in ten seconds flat, looking as neat as a new pin. (How do they do it?) If you're feeling as if you've been slung on the scrapheap of life, a Virgo will interrupt your tale of woe with a hundred handy hints and then try to find you another job.

The next thing to remember about this sign is their ceaseless search for perfection. And because they're ruled by Mercury, the planet of the mind and communication, they do this analytically. Geminis spend a lot of time thinking too, but in a swifter, more superficial way. Mercury is more practical in Virgo, restrained by the Earthy element of this sign. This quest for all things perfect means that Virgos don't suffer fools gladly; they like everything to be of the best, both materially and mentally. Sometimes this can go too far, and a Virgo will become fussy and finicky to a fanatical degree. These folk can pick holes in everything, because nothing matches up to their ideals. (But take heart, because the faults they most often find are within themselves.)

Before you've spent five minutes with vestal Virgos you'll have noticed they're naturally neat, and like things to be spick and span, and in apple-pie order. This is the sign of cleanliness, both inner and outer. With most Virgos, this means they just keep everything hunky-dory, but others can go overboard. You'd think they had disinfectant swirling through their systems, they're so obsessed about their health. (A vulnerable Virgoan will moan 'If health is wealth, then I'm broke.')

Now, you may think this sounds a bit much, and that your Virgo pals aren't like that. But they are, even if it's just in a weensy way. Next time you meet a Mercurial mate, listen carefully to the conversation. There'll be at least one reference to keeping clean or tidy, I promise, or you'll hear about their health and hygiene. (This is the sign of hypochondria!) Still not convinced? Well, next time you have a chat in a café with your chum, do a bit of brow-clutching, or seize your stomach and sigh. Say you have a headache, or that you'd better steer clear of the sausage surprise, in case it gives you one later. Your Virgo will come over all concerned, burrow into a bag or briefcase, and produce just the pill guaranteed to get you going again. (They're *that* well organised!)

When it comes to keeping their surroundings sparkling, Virgos beat everyone dusters down. If they visit you, they'll even do your tidying up, not even noticing what they're doing. There was a Virgo girl at school who was invited to more parties then all the debs in Devon, because her idea of a good time was frolicking with the Fairy Liquid in the kitchen. Put your shandy down for a second and she'd have whizzed in and whisked it away, then given the glass a good going-over in the suds in the sink. (Invite a few Virgos to your next knees-up, and you won't even have to clear away a cup – it'll all be done for you! But you've got to pick the right sort, because some of them are unutterably untidy.)

Because Virgos are usually tidy-minded and orderly, they can be somewhat sceptical and suspicious of anything they don't understand. For them, seeing is believing: they're innately inquisitive, and like to find things out for themselves. That means it's hard to pull the wool over their eyes, because they can see straight through any fast-talking. Anyone who's a fly-by-night won't stand a chance once those Mercurial minds get moving.

Virgos who make the most of their mental mastery and organisational ability can go a long way at work. (And I don't mean they make lovely long-distance lorry drivers, either!) But you might not hear about that almost certain success. Virgos are very modest, and hate blowing their own trumpets. Even when they win accolades and awards they'll prefer to keep quiet.

Unfortunately, Virgos sometimes carry this ravishing reticence into other areas of their lives. Not only will they be coy professionally, but they'll be retiring romantically, too. Their heads usually rule their hearts and Virgos can be quite cool, undemonstrative and unemotional. One Virgo relative of mine married purely for tax reasons.

This is definitely a sign that finds it hard to slow down, and Mercury makes Virgos move about like maniacs – busy bees! They can have dreadful difficulties relaxing, and will always find something to do, even if it's the dusting – for the third time in a morning. Which reminds me. I was chatting to a Mercurial male one day, and we were discussing what he'd done during Christmas. He said his girlfriend had gone to Glasgow, and left him at home. Did he mind? 'Oh no!' he grinned. 'It meant I could tidy up my flat. And I got the tops of the plugs clean. It was wonderful!' Obviously he got thirteen amps of joy from Santa that Christmas!

LIBRA – 24 SEPTEMBER–23 OCTOBER

Sugar and spice and all things nice – that's what Librans are made of. Even if you get the rare one made from puppy-dogs' tails, you can bet they'll be pretty pooches and handsome hounds. So it may come as a shock to you that this sweet, sublime sign is the iron hand in the velvet glove. 'What? Our Ethel?' I can hear you saying, but read on, my dears. Libra is a Cardinal Air sign, which means that Librans know what they want, and usually have the mental mastery to be able to get it. I mean, look at Margaret Thatcher!

Libra's ruling planet is Venus, which makes subjects of this sign courteous, charming, cheerful, caring, caressable and captivatingly cuddly. Make no mistake, loquacious Librans can charm the birdies right out of the trees when they want to. (And scintillate the squirrels while they're about it.) But if you look closely, they usually have an aim for all that charm and diplomacy.

Take a woman who has the Sun, Moon, Mars and Jupiter all in luscious Libra. (Gosh!) One day she discovered that a near-neighbour didn't give two hoots about her so she moved heaven and earth until she did, but she killed her with kindness in the process! (And piqued all her pals, who felt ignored.)

The trouble is that Librans like to be liked. In fact, they can't bear to believe that someone can't stand them. Venus can bestow beauteous bounty on her boys and girls, but sometimes she can make them too sweet for words. Even when a Libran is at his or her sugariest and sickliest, you must work out what's behind it all. Librans are assertive, ambitious and go-ahead. So they always have an end in sight. (*Votre derrière*, dear.) It could be to keep the peace (incredibly important to Librans), or to get a new job, but it will be something. Of the other Cardinal signs, Ariens will tramp through the rest of the zodiac, Cancerians will drown everyone in tears, and Capricorns will lumber along like a ten-ton tank. But Librans try to get what they want with a smile. (And they usually succeed.)

This is the sign of nuptial bliss, of partnerships of all persuasions, both in business and in love. (Committed relationships of one sort or another loom large in a Libran life.) And so it's the sign of enemies, too. After all, you can have a rapport with a rival just as much as you'll have an affinity with an amourette. The strength of the emotion is the same. Although the Libran motto is 'Peace at all costs', you mustn't forget the razor's edge between love and hate.

The polar sign of Libra is Aries, and these two can have a

wonderful relationship, because they balance each other beautifully. (And remember that though Librans, being the sign of the Scales, are always trying to achieve perfect harmony in their lives, their own set of scales can go up and down like yo-yos.) The archetypal Arien-Libran relationship is the Tarzan and Jane jamboree. There's Arien Tarzan swinging through the shrubbery, leaping about in a little loincloth, while Libran Jane stays at home being perky and pretty, probably with a little dishcloth. (Wearing it, of course, in a lovely shade of pink.) The Libran's keyword is 'You', whereas Ariens say '*Me!*' Librans can think too much of their partners and pals, to their own detriment, and can stride off through sleet and snow to minister to a mate who's ill. Some of them can be too selfless for words, although they may still be doing it for a reason – to be liked and loved!

Librans should stop being so concerned with the welfare of their loved ones, and think of themselves sometimes instead. In astrology, every sign has a positive and a negative side, and if you go to extremes in either direction it can be terrible.

This is the sign of puffy pink clouds, baby-blue angora wool and pink-and-white icing. You see, Libra is a very pretty sign indeed. It's not as fantastical and fairy-tale as the Fish, because Librans have more of a sense of reality. Nevertheless, the Libran quest is very much for beauty, and with this love for all things bright and beautiful, Librans can't cope with anything coarse, callous or crude.

The trouble with Librans is that they can be irritatingly indecisive; you can go grey while waiting for them to make up their minds about whether to feast on a fairy cake or have a blow-out on bangers and mash. (In the end you want to bash them over the bonce with the frying pan.) That may be why they're so considerate, and always ask you what *you* want to do, what *you* want to eat – because they know they haven't the foggiest idea. (Although lots of them *do* know, and try to coerce you into choosing their choice.)

They also like to keep everything fair and square, and if they feel they've been wronged, they'll fight like Aries or be as stubborn as the most intransigent Taurean to prove they're in the right. Justice must be seen to be done – in the Libran's eyes, at least. (Negative Librans will get their sense of justice a mite mixed up.) But even positive Librans will tamper with the balance they find in their lives, on their oh-so-sensitive scales, and wonder if they've got it right. ('On the other hand,' they'll sigh, 'I could be wrong.' This sort of soul-searching can go on for ever, and frequently does!)

Librans' love of harmony and balance extends to matters of the heart, as you might expect. They must have luscious lovers (they must be physically fantastic), and the Libran man must have the most beautiful bird in town in tow, even if he's as ugly as a vulture himself (though he'll have a smashing smile and delicious dimples). Accuse Librans of this and they will say in a superior way that they're an intellectual Air sign, and so plump for personality, first and foremost. But you try to get a Libran to go out with some-one who's no oil painting, but has bags of bounce and bonhomie, and see what happens. That's right. *Nothing!*

SCORPIO – 24 OCTOBER–22 NOVEMBER

Listen. Do you want to know a secret? (Where have I heard that line before?) Do you promise not to tell? Scorpios are ace! Their coolness can be captivating, and their furtiveness fascinating. And they're so laid back it's luscious!

Scorpios have more undercurrents than a conger eel. You never know what makes them tick because they never give you a clue. (Is it clockwork or quartz?) They sit looking enigmatic, and you wonder what on earth they're thinking about!

In fact, enigmatic is the supreme Scorpio word. The normal give-away for this Plutonic sign is the eyes, which are like deep pools – you wonder what's going on below the surface. Scorpios are like icebergs; after all, if you combine their element, Water, with their Fixed quality, what do you get but ice?

Aries and Scorpio share the ancient rulership of mighty Mars, yet their temperaments are as different as chalk and cheese. Ariens have flashes of Fiery fury, and act on impulse (they'll suddenly strangle you with a sock). Scorpios, though, simmer and smoulder on the back burner of life's cooker, plotting and planning how to get even with you. And they'll manage it in the end! Scorpios have psychological power, and use it to the full whenever they can. (They could manipulate Machiavelli!)

Never underestimate a Scorpio. This is a phantasmagorically profound placing for a person, and Scorpios are imbued with intensity. This is, after all, the sign of sex and death.

Death, for a Scorpio, isn't always something physical; instead these folk can kill off certain sections of their lives they no longer like in the twinkling of an eye. They can transform and transfigure their lives more than any other sign, making fresh starts with barely a backward glance. However, since this is the sign of obsessions, some Scorpios are fascinated by physical death, and can gad about graveyards, looking at the headstones and absorbing the atmosphere. They'll be engrossed and enthralled by the ritual of death, and almost have death wishes, because they can't wait to know what it's like on the other side. Other Scorpios go to the opposite extreme, and are petrified of popping off!

Make no mistake, this is a sign of such compulsion, obsession and profundity that some people find Scorpios

hard to handle. Just thinking about their intense inqui-
sitions, interrogations and investigations makes some
folk's hair stand on end! Scorpios can be like an oil rig,
drilling deep into the heart of the matter. (I wonder how
many of the men are called Derrick?) And if you want to
know what makes a Scorpio tick, you've got to do the same
to them. Then you'll start to see what's submerged beneath
that superficially serene surface. (A Scorpio may come
across as cool, calm and collected, but underneath that
elegant exterior is a sizzling selection of scorching sensations simply seething away!)

Power is very important to these Plutonians, but it's
always gained in a secretive way. Scorpios operate behind
the scenes; they love to manipulate others, but hate to be
caught in the glare of the spotlight themselves.

But don't just think there's only one sort of Scorpio,
who's like the Spanish Inquisition. There are three sides to
the sign, from the angelic to the awful. Top of the list is the
devout Dove. This is the Scorpio who believes in peace and
tranquillity, and strives for it at all costs. (Perhaps even
becoming a nun or a monk in the process.) Next comes the
exciting Eagle – the daredevil hero who takes risks and
laughs in the face of danger. Whether James or Jane Bond,
this Scorpio works behind the scenes as a spy or a secret
agent. (You can always spot 'em because they shin up
drainpipes in the dark, clutching cartons of chocs between
their teeth!) So far so good, I hear you say. But lastly comes
the sly Snake, that slithers through the undergrowth of life,
then slinks out when you least expect it, and buries its fangs
in your ankle. Ouch! These are the mass-murderers, the
Charles Mansons of the world. (No wonder Scorpios can
get a bad name!)

Luckily for the rest of us, that is the lowest level to which
a Scorpio can sink. (It's the lowest level to which anyone
can sink!) Higher-minded Scorpios choose to follow a positive path, seeking out the spiritual side of life. But a truly

negative Scorpio will turn to black magic to fulfil that pulverising passion for power, taking a macabre interest in things most people shy away from. Once you've totally understood a complex Scorpio you'll have solved one of astrology's most ancient mysteries, and be shown sensational sights of life that no other sign can offer.

SAGITTARIUS
23 NOVEMBER–21 DECEMBER

Talk about clumsy! If Sagittarians aren't putting both feet in it verbally, they're doing it physically, and landing up to their necks in trouble. If you ask an Archer round for afternoon tea, don't get out the best china. It'll only get broken. (Use some plastic plates instead.) Your Sagittarian pal will rush into the room and trip over the tea table, sending the cups and saucers flying in all directions. Then, to add insult to injury, as your mate dashes off for a dishcloth to mop up the mess, he or she will step on a cream cake and crunch it into the carpet. Still, having your residence wrecked is often better than hearing the truth about yourself, Sagittarian style. Your friend can say 'I saw someone who looked just like you yesterday.' However, before you feel pleased, and start to preen, wait for the punchline. 'Then I realised it was someone else, because you've got more spots.' See what I mean?

But let's look on the bright side – something that's second nature to our jovial pals. Sagittarians are incurable optimists (their beer bottles are always half full, never half empty), and they will inject others with their infectious enthusiasm, given half a chance. If you're feeling really down in the dumps, your Sagittarian pal will bounce up, tell you a joke or two and try to get you giggling again. Go on, give 'em a grin! Jupiter, the planet that rules these Archers, makes them magnificently merry, and they'll try to jolly everyone else along too. The terrific thing about them is that they usually succeed. You can't mooch about moping for long when there's an Archer around.

Because this is the polar sign of garrulous Gemini, Sagittarians are also blessed with the gift of the gab, and can talk the hind leg off a donkey. But there is a mighty difference between these two signs. Astrologically, Gemini is the lower-minded sign, dealing with subjects superficially and knowing a little about a lot, while Sagittarius is the opposite, full of philosophy and worldly wisdom. (In ancient mythology, the Centaur – the Sagittarius symbol – was the master of teaching and healing.) During a deep discussion with an Archer, you'll find that they're searching for the meaning of life, and will ponder on the problem all through their existence. ('What's it all about, Alfie?' is definitely the Sagittarian song!) Faiths and beliefs are all-important to Archers.

Now, it's not for nothing that Sagittarius is the sign of the Archer. There's the hunter, poised with his bow and arrow, all a-quiver, taking aim at a target. Archers do this throughout their lives (always aiming for the bull's-eye), but the trouble is they often aim too high, and miss the target by miles. They set their sights too high (literally!). Sometimes, of course, an Archer will get it right first time, but usually life to these folk is like a rerun of the Battle of Hastings, with arrows flying in all directions. (If you're called Harold, you should head for the hills!)

It's all gigantic Jupiter's doing. Because he's the largest planet in the heavens, he gives some of these Sagittarians ideas above their stations. This can be a terrific trait, because it means that the Sagittarian is always striving for better things. But some Centaurs can go to the opposite extreme and exaggerate everything they come into contact with. As a result, they get everything out of proportion; they bounce about, blowing their own bugles, believing the world can't turn without them. You see, Jupiter knows no bounds – and neither do Sagittarians. (The world doesn't just end at Ambridge for these Archers!)

This is the universal sign, and all Archers are tantalised by travel and the thought of far-flung corners of the globe. Think of the Sagittarians you know. You'll find that lots of them went round the world as soon as they could, or lived in a foreign country at some point in their lives. (Their passports contain more stamps than a Stanley Gibbons catalogue!) This desire to get out and see the world for themselves can be the making of positive Sagittarians. Negative Archers, though, can wax lyrical about their exotic adventures, name-dropping like mad, so it sounds as though they spent a weekend at the White House, when actually they only whizzed past it on a bus.

Jupiter is the planet of luck and opportunity, and some Archers are just like cats, with nine lives. (Some of them are so accident-prone, they need all the help they can get!) You may think they're gauche and rude, but they call it being honest! They make the most of every opportunity that arises, and can often spot a chance when others don't think it's there. Sometimes that'll be their brilliant perception and vision, and other times it'll be blind faith and living in cloud-cuckoo-land. It's up to the Archer to decipher the mystical Morse code.

Meet a positive Sagittarian and you will be fulfilled in many ways, and imbued with a zest and a zeal for living. But a negative Archer can be crafty, or will let you down in some way or other, whether emotionally or materially. These folk can waste everyone's time, and will bite off more than they can chew. All Sagittarians need challenges; they need to know where to aim their celestial bows and arrows so they can hit the target fair and square. After all, it's much better to climb the ladder of life, rung by rung, than to take a flying leap at it and miss by miles!

CAPRICORN – 22 DECEMBER–20 JANUARY

Right, repeat after me, 'Capricorns are captivating.' Say it again. Got it? Good. Now remember it, and forget what you might have heard about these folk being morose and melancholic. You will find some Goats with a grouse, because there are positive and negative folks in every sign, but a together Goat can be gorgeous.

Let's get the worst over first with this sign. Some Capricorns can be the original wet blankets, moaning and misanthropic, complaining and carping, and generally being gloomy old things. You'll look at them and think 'I don't want to know you.' But if you bother to get to know them, you can have the time of your life. Talk about giggle!

One of the tremendous traits of this bunch is their superb sense of humour and wit that's as dry as a bone, but much more fun. They can take the mickey out of everything – including themselves, which makes them very endearing indeed. And they really do act the goat, making you laugh until your sides split. Once you've glimpsed the sensational side of this sign, you can turn a blind eye to its more *triste* traits, because you'll have found the silver lining to the Capricorn cloud. (And the crock of gold at the end of the rainbow, if the Goat has Taurus rising.)

Some negative Capricorns can pick holes in everything – even if they hit the jackpot at bingo, they'll moan about having to spend all that money. The poor things can't express their emotions, either, and will bottle up all their feelings and frustrations.

When you meet a Capricorn, expect them to act older than their years. Goats age in the opposite way to the rest of us, behaving as if they were fifty when they're only five, and seven when they're seventy. This means that Capricorns make elderly-seeming babies and young-at-heart pensioners. When the rest of us are being put out to grass, Goats are just coming into their own!

This is a sign that believes in experience, with a capital 'E'. They never have an easy life until they've blown out all the candles on their thirtieth birthday cakes. Until then, life will have been one long struggle; the only way for them to survive is to learn by experience. (Capricorns hate wasting *anything*!) Many of them will have had cramped childhoods, awful adolescences and terrible twenties. But they'll have terrific thirties, fantastic forties – even naughty nineties!

There are two types of Goat – the ones who cavort and curvet up the crags to the summit of their own mountain-sides, and the ones who are domestic, and like to potter about their own pieces of pasture, never straying far from the fireside. Capricorns are Cardinal, making them astoundingly ambitious, and even the domestic ones will be determined to do well. Success for them, though, isn't totally based on boodle (although they'd never refuse owt for nowt!); honour, public position and status all smell sweet to them.

Capricorns need security, which they get from the tried, true and tested. They love history, and anything with a past (this could mean you), because then they feel safe. Capricorns are conservative, canny and cautious, and are suspicious of new-fangled things, until they get used to them. They hate to fly in the face of convention.

They're very wary of wearing out their wallets, too. They believe that if they take care of the farthings, the pennies will look after themselves. More positive Goats would call themselves careful, and will be generous with their loot when they've got it, and laugh about it when they haven't. (Always with a note of caution in their grin!)

Guilt is a very Goaty thing, and some Capricorns thrive on it, putting everyone through the mill, including them-selves. They can set themselves impossibly high ideals, and almost galactic goals, and then hate themselves when they fail to reach them. Because just as they hate waste, they also can't abide failure. (It's a good job they're imbued with endurance and endeavour!) They are deeply determined and disciplined, so can drive themselves to hit heights others only dream of.

But not all Goats are quite so positive. Some delight in the doldrums, like grumpy old Eeyore in *Winnie the Pooh* – a donkey who's always down in the dumps. But still everyone adored him. In fact, with a little understanding, you are sure to have fun with even the most morose Goats: laugh with them, but never at them, and you'll never feel down!

AQUARIUS – 21 JANUARY–19 FEBRUARY

You learn a whole new vocabulary when you meet an Aquarian. Forget about the usual words, and ponder on ones like 'contrary', 'bizarre', 'radical' and 'outrageous'. In fact, you'd do well to remember them, because you're going to need them.

Before I go any further, let's get one thing straight. Well, two if you're going to be pedantic. (And if you are, make sure it's not in front of an Aquarian. They aren't particularly pleased by pedantic people.) There are two types of Aquarians: those ruled by Saturn and those ruled by Uranus. It's strange, I know, but then a lot of people think Aquarians are strange . . . (Watch it, because I'm one of them.)

Saturn is the ancient ruler of Aquarius; when rebellious, revolutionary Uranus was revealed, he was given to the Sun sign most fitting that description – Airy Aquarius. (Some people think Aquarius is a Water sign, but it isn't. Its symbol may be the Water Carrier, but it is actually the third of the Air signs. Confusing, isn't it?)

Saturn Aquarians tend to be conservative, reliable and positive pillars of proper society. You won't catch them wearing lampshades for hats, unless you've spiked their

31

sherry. If that sounds a bit like Capricorn, you're right. Saturn Aquarians do have a lot of Capricorn's characteristics, so if you think you know one, turn back to the previous chapter and have a gander at the Goats.

I'm going to deal mostly with Uranus-ruled Aquarians here. (Usually, you will discover which planet is strongest by studying the birth chart. Sometimes it will be easier – you may meet an Aquarian who is so Saturnine it's not true, or so unusual that they have to be Uranian. Unless they're just plain mad.)

An ancient astrological adage says you can't tell Aquarians anything because they know it already, and very often will tell you so. One of the negative qualities of Aquarians is their one-upmanship. You can meet an Aquarian mate for a meal, and arrive in a wheelchair with your bonce in a big bandage. As the waiter whizzes you to the table, you will smile through your layers of lint, expecting a sudden show of sympathy. The Aquarian will look up, and ask you what happened. So far so good. After you've mumbled in a muffled manner that you were weeding your window box and fell off, fracturing your femur and splitting your skull, the Aquarian will sigh, say 'Oh, is that all?' and go on to recount how they once broke both arms *and* both legs, wrecked their ribs and biffed their back, while morris dancing at Kew Gardens. It can make you mad, but don't kick them with your cast, because it'll hurt you more than them. The negative Saturn Aquarian can be like the negative Capricorn, and be plagued with pessimism, downcast by depression and doubt, and worn out with worry.

The two halves of Aquarius are so very different. If the Saturn type is black and white, then the Uranian Aquarian is all the colours in the spectrum. They can be completely confusing, contrary, unpredictable and incomprehensible – qualities that set them completely apart from their Saturn brothers and sisters. Uranus Aquarians are all of a jitter, rushing here and there, and constantly changing their moods. They remind me of Merlin, popping up when you least expect it. In astrology, Uranus is known as the great awakener, as if a magic wand had been waved, the word 'abracadabra' said. He will create change in something that was static. So, the Uranus-ruled Aquarian is ceaselessly craving change.

On a positive level, this means that the Aquarian is eternally excited and exhilarated by what may lie round the corner, and there may be sudden changes of career, luck or partners when Uranus decides to stage a shake-up. Negatively, an Aquarian will want to change things just for the sake of it, because he or she longs to rock the boat. Routine can be anathema to an Aquarian; the Saturn Aquarian, on the other hand, may find it rather reassuring. This is the quintessence of the Aquarian quandary – complete contradiction, with one half of the sign panting for pastures new, and the other following the furrow.

You never know what's going to happen next with an Aquarian. Life can be a lot of fun, or you can find it very tiring. Aquarians are unconventional, but they are also original, and along with Geminis, are said to be the geniuses of the zodiac. They can be inventive and brilliantly clever, although sometimes they are spectacular in such a strange way, so abstract and off at such a tremendous tangent, that no one knows what they're talking about! Aquarians are really born way ahead of their time. (After all, they laughed at Christopher Columbus when he said the world was round!) Other people, who are rather less free-thinking and original, will conclude that they are completely cranky.

Another Aquarian contradiction is that although Water Carriers are said to be humanitarians, they can be emotional ice cubes in the cocktail of life, and don't easily express their emotions. They *can* be humanitarian – helping others, sending cash to charities, or being affectionate on a large scale – yet find their own close relationships difficult to cope with. Aquarius is a Fixed sign, so it can be intolerably inflexible and intransigent. For all their brainpower and brilliance, Aquarians can be staggeringly stupid and stubborn, standing their ground over a long-lost cause and unable to admit they are in the wrong.

Since Aquarius is an Air sign, the Aquarian will be much more mesmerised by a marriage of the minds than a partnership of passion and physical fulfilment. Very often, they pick the most unlikely-looking person for a partner, because they will have chosen them for their mind rather than for anything else. Aquarians can have some very avant-garde relationships! (Ever heard of Beauty and the beast? And guess who's playing Beauty!)

Aquarians think of the future a great deal; often when they have just crossed one hurdle, they will think 'Where will this lead?' and 'I wonder what's going to happen next?' And this brings me to another Aquarian attribute. They are the only sign to answer a question with a question. Ask an Aquarian if it's raining, and he or she will ask you why you want to know. (A Piscean would say yes, and offer to lend you their green gamp.) The first word Aquarian children learn is 'Why?', and they will continue to ask that question all through their lives.

You can never get really close to an Aquarian. Unless they have plenty of Pisces and Taurus in their charts to warm them up, they can be aloof and cold and difficult to cuddle. But for all that, life with an Aquarian, either as a pal or a partner, will never be dull, and that's something to think about!

PISCES – 20 FEBRUARY–20 MARCH

Saintly Pisces! Some of these Fish should be canonised, they are so far advanced along the road to spiritual enlightenment. (Others still seem to be waiting at the heavenly bus stop!)

Now, there are two sorts of Pisceans; this last sign of the zodiac is ruled by two planets – jocular, jaunty Jupiter, and nebulous, nectarine Neptune. The Jupiter-ruled Pisceans are very akin to Sagittarians, because they share the same ruler. But Jupiterian Pisceans aren't prone to the flights of fancy shown by Sagittarians. Their ruler represents wealth and good fortune, and the Jupiterian Fish will always have an eye on these things. In fact, Pisces brings out these Jupiterian qualities beautifully, making the Fish full of fun and clever at bringing in the boodle. Negatively, there will be a tendency towards overexpansion, whether in girth, mirth, or wheeling and dealing. But these Jupiterian Fish do burst with bounteous bonhomie, and can be gloriously generous and marvellously magnanimous.

Because of the saintly side of this sign, Pisceans can be very devout and pious. (It depends on the Fish whether that will make you awed or bored.) If they are ruled by Jupiter, they will accept the faith or religion they have been brought up in. A Neptunian Piscean, however, will be more unusual, even mystical, and may find Eastern religions especially attractive.

This is a profoundly psychic sign, and the Piscean should use this ability positively to live a better life. Many Fish become fascinated by black magic and the occult, like Scorpios, because they are seduced by secrecy. But, generally, Pisceans have an inspiration that can draw them wholeheartedly into the realms of the positive supernatural and mystical. They are also intensely interested in spiritualism, because it helps them to get in touch with that unseen lot they feel so much a part of.

Neptunian Pisceans waft along on clouds, daydreaming away to their heart's content. They really aren't part of this world at all! (This isn't the same as Aquarians, who are futuristic, and one step ahead of everyone else. Pisceans are unworldly in a filigree, fantasial way.) These Fish will appear magical and mystical, and they can be profoundly artistic and unworldly sometimes, to the point of being gullible or geniuses. Lord Byron had powerful Piscean placings, and Mozart and Chopin both had the Sun in this sign, as did Rudolph Nureyev, who brought a whole new concept to ballet. (And to tights. Pisceans love to leave something to the imagination!)

What you must remember about Neptune is that this planet gives an illusory image to everything it encounters. Neptune represents something that can never be captured or held on to. Think of an intangible will-o'-the-wisp, or a piece of thistledown floating through the air that always eludes you, and you have the perfect picture of Pisceans.

They can bring this quality into their everyday lives, imbuing them with illusion, and smothering them in strange sea mists. You will think you're looking at one thing, then the shadows shift and you discover you're seeing something quite different.

Everything that Neptune does is intensified in an ethereal way, so Neptunian Pisceans will be hypersensitive, and as fragile as a butterfly's wing. They can feel neurotically nauseated by anything ugly, whether it's society, sights, sounds or situations. Some Fishy folk can't stand the slightest facial flaw, let alone anything else. (Better talk to them with your head hidden!) Yet such is their spiritual self-awareness, that often they will devote their lives to the very vocations which you'd think they couldn't bear. For example, they might join the prison service (but not behind bars!), look after the old and infirm, and the mentally and physically handicapped. These positive Pisceans force themselves to face up to their phobias, and bring some good out of them. (Other Pisceans will only want the erotic, exotic, seductive and sumptuous side of life, and none of the unpleasant parts.)

I can hear you saying 'That sounds like Libra!', and you'd

be right. Neptune is said to be the higher octave of Venus, a sort of top C of the zodiac. It's like a dog whistle, which has a note that's too high for humans to hear. And this is what Neptunian natives are like – they're listening to a high-pitched tone that the rest of us can't catch. Equally, Jupiter is said to be the higher octave of Mercury, and Jupiterian folk can understand all the deeper things of life that a Mercury-ruled person skims over. Between them, Mercury and Jupiter rule the four Mutable signs – Gemini, Virgo, Sagittarius and Pisces. (Interesting, isn't it?)

Neptune is a fantastically fantasial figure. On a positive level, its influence means that Neptunians can be wonderful writers, divine dancers and profound poets. (And incurable romantics.) But negatively, they can be monstrously Machiavellian, playing one person off against another. Some of them make Lucrezia Borgia look like Little Bo Peep; they can be malicious and malevolent, vicious and venomous, treacherous and two-faced. (They have a wonderful way of believing their own fibs and fables.) And this is how we get the symbol of Pisces, which is a fish swimming in different directions. Pisceans are either way up at the top of the tree or at rock bottom; either the nurse helping the drug addict or the addict himself.

Fish are vulnerable, and can be victims of the unknown, murky depths of their imaginations and subconscious minds. They are either inspired, or they're the dregs of the earth, who rely on society to look after them.

There's no getting away from it. This sign is a mystery, but not in a Scorpionic way. Rather, it's unworldly, in a delicious, delectable, gossamer-like way. There is a floaty, flimsy veil hiding what is really going on in the Piscean life. The Fish can inhabit a very weird world, and the worst thing Pisceans can do is to drift along on an aimless sea, when their phobias, fetishes and fixations may well get the better of them. They are very impressionable indeed, and negative Pisceans will be plagued by psychosomatic problems that they have brought on themselves. Positive Pisceans can direct that abundant artistry, that magnificent mysticism, into a brilliant conclusion. Or they can live such serene spiritual lives that nothing else matters, because their tremendous inner peace brings them total fulfilment.

Think of your Fishy friends, and you'll realise that something strange sets them apart from everyone else. You can't put your finger on it, but you know it's there. Remember those sea mists. One minute the view is as clear as a bell, the next you're sinking into a ferocious fog! It's a magical, mystical mystery.

RUSSELL'S RELATIONSHIP GUIDE

CAPRICORN MAN AND ARIES WOMAN

Ambitions could be the biggest bond between the two of you, because you're both Cardinal creatures and know exactly what you want from life. What's more, you're both determined to go out and get it! If you both share the same aim of being together forever, though, you might have to resolve a few problems first. For a start, your egos could clash so loudly they sound like a pair of false teeth clicking away, and your cautious and conservative ways may drive your adventurous Arien round the bend – she's much more slap-dash and relaxed about life than you. Money may make ripples or even tidal waves between you, as your Martian maiden believes in lavishing the loot in all directions, whilst you prefer to count every penny before committing yourself. Never mind, because when it comes to the passion ration, you're both imbued with enormous helpings of sexy urges and surges that will help to patch up any problems between you.

CAPRICORN MAN AND TAURUS WOMAN

You're the tops! Whether it's business or pleasure, you two go together like champagne and caviare – or bread and water if you're feeling broke! As you're both Earth signs you understand what makes each other tick, and your Taurean amour needs the material possessions that you can give her once you've achieved your ambition of reaching the top of the tree. Along the way you'll dole out help and encouragement to one another, and if you've formed a business double act than you'll soon be laughing all the way to the bank! Money always plays a large part in your partnership, even if it's under the surface, as financial independence is something you both need. Another thing that your Bullette craves is emotional security, and you're just the chap to give her oodles of it! You may not deluge her with hearts and flowers, but you've got some very sensual and sentimental ways of showing that you care!

CAPRICORN MAN AND GEMINI WOMAN

Naughty but nice! That's the sexual scenario when you two pair up, and you'll get up to all sorts of tantalising and titillating tricks together. (Your Gemini girl will soon discover why Capricorn is the sign of the Goat!) Because you're a mite old-fashioned, you'll revel in being the head of the household and bringing home the bacon, especially if there's enough loot left over to let you live off the fat of the land! Who's complaining? Certainly not you! Having fun and frolics will keep your sex life spicy and saucy and stop you seeing it all as a dreary duty. You may be hard-working, but if you turn into a workaholic who's more besotted with your briefcase than your beloved, your Mer-curial maid will feel fed up fast and decide to get her own back by painting the town every colour of the rainbow. If you suspect anything, she can always dream up a good excuse and cover her tracks!

CAPRICORN MAN AND CANCER WOMAN

The more security you two can bring to your lives, the happier you'll be! That may not mean putting bolts on all the doors, but it will mean instilling each other with a strong sense of being cherished, cosy, cosseted and cared for, especially through sex, which can be imbued with magnificent meaning. If you set up home together, you'll want to spend as much time as you can cuddled up in your wee nest, especially if there's a baby or two to carry on the family name. The only thing to watch is if you turn into a working wonder who's never at home, because then your Cancerian Cupid will feel neglected, left out and very unhappy indeed. What's more, she'll show her hurt feelings by being clingy, carping and crabby, and you'll respond by being stern, silent and sullen. Don't let things get to this un-pretty pass and you'll be a delightful duo.

CAPRICORN MAN AND LEO WOMAN

Businesswise it's brill when you two join forces, but romantically it could be another story, and not necessarily one that ends happily ever after! You see, your feelings are at opposite ends of the emotional spectrum, and whilst your Leo lass is demonstrative and believes in displaying her affections, you may prefer to keep a stiff upper lip and not betray a flicker of feeling. Woe betide your Leo love if she flings her arms round you in public or gives you a smacking kiss in front of your kith and kin, and after a while she could feel very fed up with having to restrain her romancing. What's more, you could soon see sex as just one of the many duties you have to perform, and your hot-blooded Lioness won't take kindly to that at all! She also won't appreciate the way you seem wedded to your work as well as her, and though she'll love enjoying the fruits of your labours, she won't want to be a grass widow for long. Better do some straight talking before she decides there are plenty more fish in the sea.

CAPRICORN MAN AND VIRGO WOMAN

It's a perfect pairing! Or is it? If your Virgoette is the sort of girl who believes in service with a smile, then she'll be happy ever after with you, but she could change her mind pretty pronto if you're the sort of chauvinist Capricorn who thinks a woman's place is in the home. Are you climbing the ladder of success slowly but surely? Then your Virgoan valentine will be happy to help you in any way she can, whether it's cleaning your clothes or cooking a big blow-out for the boss, but she'll draw the line if you start taking advantage of her or spend more time in the boardroom than your bedroom. Your sexual shenanigans can be very bawdy and boisterous indeed, though at the slightest hint of anything really dirty she'll be on her hands and knees – with the scrubbing brush!

CAPRICORN MAN AND LIBRA WOMAN

If Cupid's wee bow and arrow has made you fall for a Libran lass, then be warned. It's love that's brought you together, but it's also love that could tear you apart. You see, your Libran love needs a daily dose of devotion from her darling, but you may find it hard to keep doling out your portion of passion. Her name may be engraved on your titanic ticker for ever more, but you'd rather go through fire and brimstone than say so. If she longs for Moons and Junes, romantic rendezvous and sentimental journeys down memory lane then I'm afraid that she's picked the wrong chap. Instead, you'll probably grab her in a funny place and start running through an erotic repertoire that makes the *Kama Sutra* look like a book for beginners. Your Libran lady may find that a bit too much but if you can come to a real understanding you'll do your utmost to make each other happy. Now, you can't say fairer than that!

CAPRICORN MAN AND SCORPIO WOMAN

'Heaven, I'm in heaven.' You usually try to be practical and pragmatic, but once you've paired up with a Scorpio siren then you'll be singing songs, skipping and dancing like there's no tomorrow. What's making you so happy? Well, you hate the thought of being rejected by the one you love, but when your amour is as emotional, intense and serious-minded as this Scorpionette then you've got nowt to worry about. If you want to carve out a career and aim for the top of your professional tree, then you'll be pleased to know that she's behind you all the way, urging you on to greater things and keeping the home fires burning. Both of you are faithful folk, so unless something goes wrong there'll be no worries about one of you running off with a new amour. Your pulsating Plutonian's passions will really get you going, and the temperature could reach boiling point in the bedroom. Wow!

CAPRICORN MAN AND SAGITTARIUS WOMAN

Bring on the dancing girls! You'll have a high old time when you fall for a Sagittarian lady, especially if you're determined to make your mark on the world. Let's face it, she adores an *homme* who's building up a big bank balance or improving his prestige, and if you're a canny Capricorn then you're almost bound to be doing both. What fun you'll have going on spending sprees or meeting VIPs and any other influential folk you bring home, especially if it means she can put on a splendid and slap-up show! There's only one snag – if you're both waiting for all that luck, loot and luxury just to land in your laps, then you could be in for a rude awakening. What's more, if you're the sort of Capricorn who's a Scrooge or stinge-pot, then you certainly won't share your Saggy sweetheart's easy come, easy go attitude to affluence and could decide to padlock your purse and refuse to part with a penny more than you have to. Don't let money come between you.

CAPRICORN MAN AND CAPRICORN WOMAN

For better, for worse – that's the motto for your relationship once you pair up with a fellow Goat. Let's face it, you've both got oodles of staying power, so even if your partnership hits a problematic patch, your sex life peters out into the odd cuddle or you're low on loot, you won't dream of parting company in the search for better times elsewhere. Instead, you'll stick it out together, linked by loyalty and the determination to make your liaison a success. You see, you share the same aims and ambitions, and if you both want to reach the top rung on the ladder of success, then you'll be behind each other all the way and offer any help or advice that's necessary. Respect will play a large part in your life together, and you'll have a magnificent and munificent mutual admiration society. Some couples who share the same sign can hit hassles and hiccups, but that isn't the case for this accomplished alliance!

CAPRICORN MAN AND AQUARIUS WOMAN

Before you go any further, better find out whether your Aquarian amour is ruled by unruly Uranus or sane Saturn. If she's motivated by that perplexing planet Uranus, then your relationship could be about as exciting as a damp squib, because you just won't understand each other one bit. On the other hand, if your womanly Water Carrier is strongly Saturnine, then she'll be quite Capricorn in her character, although she'll still act the Aquarian and take you by surprise sometimes. You'll be as happy as sandboys and sandgirls together, and sexually things will go with a real swing, but if your amour is truly Uranian then you could both give up in disgust and read a good book instead! You just won't have anything in common, and your sober and sensible ways will clash catastrophically with her avant-garde and original approach to life. It could all be very difficult to deal with.

CAPRICORN MAN AND PISCES WOMAN

Perfection! You make a delightful duo, and you'll love being in each other's company. What makes this such a magnificent match is that you can each offer what the other one wants. As a Capricorn chap you're the strong, sensible and steadfast sort, which is just what your Fishy female needs from the love of her life. She'll adore knowing that you're loyal to a fault and the fact that you'll never neglect your family responsibilities and duties will fill her with a stronger sense of safety and satisfaction. In return, she'll refine and reform you if you're a coarse Capricorn, and teach you to appreciate the finer feelings and the more ethereal and spiritual side of life. In the boudoir, you'll have a field day, as both of you love getting up to kinky capers and the sort of physical fun and games that you never learnt in the school gym! Cope with any problematic patches in the early stages of your relationship and you'll have a smashing set-up.

CAPRICORN WOMAN AND ARIES MAN

Whoops a daisy! There could be clashes and conflicts galore when you meet an Arien chap. Money could come high on the list of problems, as he likes splashing it about in all directions, whilst you like to have every penny accounted for. It can drive you round the bend! If you want this partnership to work, you've got to take a leaf out of each other's books, so your Martian male learns more about saving, and you take a crash course in spending. Another big bonus would be if you could set up in business together, cashing in on your burning ambitions to make successes of yourselves. That way, you could go very far indeed, although you'll get embroiled in big battles about how to do things (you both believe that your way is best!). Never mind, because you're laughing when it comes to sex – you're both randy, rampant and rapacious, so it's the perfect pairing passionwise!

CAPRICORN WOMAN AND TAURUS MAN

Money talks when you two get together. In fact, it speaks volumes! You're both very concerned about cash, and once you've discovered that you both think along the same financial lines, with no dangers that one of you will run off with the proceedings of the piggy bank or joint account, then you'll both be in clover. (You've got to get your priorities right!) As you're both Earth signs, there's a deliciously sensual and seductive feel to all amorous encounters that will keep both of you happy and content, and you'll bring out all sorts of sensations and sentiments that neither of you knew about. You're just as good in the boardroom as the bedroom, 'cos you make brill business partners, with your boy Bull able to keep a firm grip on the boodle and you good at masterminding the whole operation. Your perfect pairing can lead to prestige and profit as well as passion, and you can't say fairer than that!

CAPRICORN WOMAN AND GEMINI MAN

Difficult but delightful! That could be the story of your romance if you're lucky, but even so this is a pairing that's peppered with problems and pitfalls. You see, as a glamorous Goat you can be sensationally sophisticated, sassy and sexy on the surface, but underneath what you're really looking for is security – and that could be the last thing your Gemini chap is prepared to give you! Because he's a Mercurial male he adores being on the loose, but it'll go down like a lead balloon when he tries telling you that he isn't ready to make any emotional commitments. You'll only feel happy when you know that you're two hearts beating as one, and even when you've tied the knot you could come on far too strong for your Gemini man. Claustrophobia could be just around the corner! Even so, he'll love the way you make heads turn, and your smashing sense of humour will keep him chuckling for a long time to come.

CAPRICORN WOMAN AND CANCER MAN

Memories are made of this, and what ravishing recollections they'll be! Once you two pair up you'll wonder why you were ever apart (you'll forget that it's because you didn't know each other!), and if things go well you'll swear never to let each other out of your sight ever again. Not that there's any danger of that, 'cos you'll be almost as close as a couple of Siamese twins! Being Cardinal creatures, you're both very ambitious and determined to achieve what you want from life, so spur each other on and soon profit, prominence, prestige and pleasure could be yours. The only possible problem is if you both want to reach the top of your professional or prestigious trees, because you could start competing with each other and having hassles over who wears the trousers at home. Get that sartorial snag sorted out and you'll be a winning team!

CAPRICORN WOMAN AND LEO MAN

'Hey, good looking!' That's what your Leo lad will say when he first claps eyes on sleek, soignée and sophisticated you (unless you're one of the few girl Goats who looks as though they've been pulled through a hedge backwards, in which case he may not even give you the time of day). As a proud Leo lad, he loves having a decorative damsel on his arm, and he couldn't have picked a better bet than you. The problems will start (yes, I know there always seems to be a snag!) when things switch from being social to sexual, as you may be very reserved when it comes to romance. Your Leo love will have to be patient if you find it hard to let your hair down, all because you're worried about committing yourself to someone and then being rejected. It could take a lot of hard work to win your trust and your heart, but once he's got them you can both begin building a relationsip that'll last for ever and a day.

CAPRICORN WOMAN AND VIRGO MAN

What a sensational set-up! Once you two get together you'll wonder how you ever survived apart, because you could have been made for each other. You both belong to the Earthy element of the astrological arrangement, making you deliciously down to earth and diligent, and filling you with respect and reverence for each other. You've got stacks in common sexually too, and can look forward to a very raunchy, randy and rapacious relationship. What you two get up to within your own four walls can defy description! No matter what your Mercurial male does for a living, you'll be behind him all the way, doling out some sensible and sound advice whenever it's needed and giving him oodles of encouragement. What's more, you've got a very ambitious streak and could conduct a career of your own that swells the coffers and fills your Virgo chap with pride and pleasure. You're definitely the dame for him!

CAPRICORN WOMAN AND LIBRA MAN

Smashing! You're both Cardinal creatures so you share a need to achieve your ambitions, and you'll be behind each other one hundred per cent, whatever you turn your hand to. What's more, if your Libran lad wants to bring the boss home for dinner, he can rest assured that you'll be on your very best behaviour and do him proud. Sexually, though, it could be the very other way round, with you letting your hair down in a very extreme, erotic and exotic way, whilst he goes all hot and cold with embarrassment and wonders what on earth you're going to get up to next. (And you could have some very outré and unusual games up your sleeve!) You'll be close emotionally and able to show your feelings for each other, but there could be a big sexual gap between you that's hard to cross.

CAPRICORN WOMAN AND SCORPIO MAN

What a tremendous twosome! Whether you're friends, family or partners in passion, you two get on swimmingly, helped by the fact that you've got loads in common. Because neither of you likes relationships that are over as

48

soon as they've begun, once you fall in love you'll want to stay together forever. After all, you share the same need for emotional security and you like to know where you stand with your other half, so there'll be no problems with you two. As a Scorpio, your darling's desires can be very strong and sultry, but you won't mind that one bit. You may look a cool, calm and collected Capricornette on the surface but once you slip between the sheets you could show your Scorpio sweetheart a thing or two! As long as he remembers to treat you as a woman in your own right and not just as a sex symbol, then as the years go by your love will grow and grow. It sounds like a delightful prospect!

CAPRICORN WOMAN AND SAGITTARIUS MAN
Talk about teamwork! When you two pair up you can devise a fantastic formula that ensures your success, whether personally or professionally. Your Sagittarian man always aims high, and there's nothing you like better than achieving your ambitions – or backing those of your inamorata. Now, your idealistic Archer isn't very good at tying up the loose ends of his projects, so he'll be delighted if you tidy up after him and set the seal of success on all his dealings. Together, you could go very far indeed. He may like to be footloose and fancy-free, but if you're clever, you'll let him swan off on his travels, knowing that he'll soon return to your side. There's just one thing – make sure your liaison is based on more than just lust, otherwise when it wears off you'll find that there's nothing to keep you together. You wouldn't want that, would you?

CAPRICORN WOMAN AND CAPRICORN MAN
Only the best is good enough when you join forces with a Capricorn chap! Neither of you could be accused of being spendthrifts, squanderers or splurgers (you rate loot far too highly for that!), but even so you'll only part with your hard-earned cash when you know you're getting value for

money. You share the same sentiments and emotional needs, and there could be plenty of lust and love in your liaison. (What a pair of old Goats!) Even if you're partners who are more platonic than passionate, your faithfulness and constancy will mean you'd rather be together than off with other folk. The only fly in the ointment will come if one of you is supremely successful whilst the other is an out-and-out failure, as then there could be recriminations, jealousy and all sorts of undesirable feelings seething under the surface. But if you share the limelight you'll be able to bask in its warmth, as well as the glow of knowing you're the perfect companions.

CAPRICORN WOMAN AND AQUARIUS MAN
What a dynamic duo! As long as you don't get bogged down in tradition, ruts or routines, the two of you could have a grand time together. If your Aquarian amour is strongly Saturnine then you'll find you've got stacks in common, but even if he's a Uranian *homme* it won't be the end of the world. Try to take his controversial, contrary and cranky characteristics in your stride, and don't turn into a clinging vine emotionally or you'll find you're left all alone. If you've fallen for a Saturnian swain then he'll have lots of Capricorn traits, but don't forget that he loves a whiff of excitement, and if there's none to be found then he'll do something outrageous just to see what will happen. You could find your eyebrows shoot straight off your head at some of the antics he gets up to, but one thing's for sure – he'll keep you laughing.

CAPRICORN WOMAN AND PISCES MAN
Now, don't take this the wrong way, but if you're a bit of a bossy-boots then this could be a very tricky twosome indeed. You're not keen on meek or mild men, but your assertive and no-nonsense ways could turn your Fishy fella into a jumpy jellyfish who'll hide his head in the sand rather

than risk your wrath. Ideally, he should be able to stand up for himself so he can give as good as he gets. Things will be much easier if you're an easy-going girl Goat and he's a Piscean with a bit of backbone, and you could spend the rest of your lives together in happy and heavenly harmony. You'll adore the sensitive and sympathetic feelings of your Fishy amour, and he'll always remember your anniversaries and think up lots of little ways to show that you're loved. Just like a fine wine, the longer the liaison lasts, the better and more blissful it will be. Now there's something to look forward to!

JUPITER AND YOU

Want to know what's best for you in the annum ahead? Keen to capitalise on every chance that comes your way, liaise with Lady Luck and let fortuosity be your guide? Then look no further, for here is your passport to prosperity, pleasure, positivity and productivity over the coming year!

It's all thanks to gigantic Jupiter, who's the superstar of the skies when it comes to bringing you luck, loot and opportunities galore. This generous planet rules two Sun signs – the Fire sign of Sagittarius and the Water sign of Pisces (which is also ruled by nebulous Neptune).

Astrologically speaking, Jupiter is linked to knowledge, expansion (whether of the brain or the belt!), travel (especially abroad), intellectual pursuits, gambling, large lumps of loot, religious beliefs and philosophical subjects. Folk with a strong Jupiter in their celestial make-up (such as the Sun, Moon or Ascendant in Sagittarius or Pisces) can be entrepreneurs, have a powerfully positive approach to life, are jovial, loyal, benevolent and blessed with inspired intellectual powers. On the other hand, anyone with negative Jupiterian traits may be overoptimistic, never know when to say no, have extremist beliefs, be conceited and be suffused with self-indulgence. The parts of the body ruled by Jupiter are the liver (which is why folk with strong Sagittarian or Piscean birth charts often get worse hangovers than other people), pituitary gland and thighs.

This personable planet takes about twelve years to complete his orbit around the zodiac, and although that sounds as though he spends a year in each sign he actually whizzes through some signs and lingers for a long time in others. If you've read my Day-by-Day Horoscope books in the past, you'll be used to seeing a long list of a particular planet's progress through the annum ahead, so don't be too surprised when you see the section showing the wee wanderings of jovial Jupiter in 1994. He may only switch signs once, but even so his astrological antics will have a profound effect on the good fortune you can expect in the year ahead. So, read on and discover how to cash in on the treasure trove of luck, opportunity and enjoyment that beckons in 1994.

JUPITER'S ENTRY INTO THE SIGNS IN 1994

from 1 January   Scorpio
9 December   Sagittarius

JUPITER'S PROGRESS THROUGH THE ZODIAC

It's as easy as pie to plot the progress of jocular Jupiter through the celestial skies with the help of my chart. The zodiac is made up of twelve houses, and each one is ruled by a particular Sun sign. When giant Jupiter arrives in your Sun sign (once every twelve years), he's said to be in your first house, then when he moves on to the next sign he's in your second house, and so on until he's travelled right round the zodiac and arrived back in your Sun sign, roughly twelve years later.

Each time he changes houses and signs, Jupiter influences a different part of your life. For instance, whenever he visits your Sun sign (your first house), he triggers off an exciting new cycle in your life and imbues all your personal affairs with his very own blend of starluck, success and satisfaction. When he dwells in a sign that's compatible with yours (which means your third, fifth, ninth and eleventh houses), you'll be riding on the crest of a wowee wave, but when he occupies a sign that isn't amenable to yours (in other words, the fourth, seventh and tenth houses), you could be too clever for your own good, find that your finances are stretched or become too big for your boots.

Using the picture of the zodiac wheel below, write in the number 1 by your Sun sign and continue in an anti-clockwise direction around the signs until you've completed them all. Then it will be easy for you to chart the progress of prosperous Jupiter over the annum ahead. Good luck!

Astrological houses numbered for someone born with the Sun in Gemini.

Fill in this diagram to plot the course of Jupiter through your astrological houses. Simply write the number 1 by your Sun sign and continue in an anti-clockwise direction until you have completed all twelve.

You probably know the symbols for the Sun signs, but I've listed them here just in case.

♈	Aries	♎	Libra
♉	Taurus	♏	Scorpio
♊	Gemini	♐	Sagittarius
♋	Cancer	♑	Capricorn
♌	Leo	♒	Aquarius
♍	Virgo	♓	Pisces

JUPITER IN YOUR FIRST HOUSE

Congratulations! You're about to embark on a voyage of searching self-discovery, in which you'll be able to explore your own potential, prospects and preconceptions. Even if you're usually shy and self-contained, you'll be able to break out of your shell now, for this is the time to bring your personality to the fore and let folk discover who and what you really are. All the same, take care you don't go overboard and blow your own trumpet so loud and long that you put people off instead of winning them over to your side! All you need do is just be yourself, so forget about putting on airs and graces or pretending to be something or someone you're not, and you'll be fine. Something else to watch is patting yourself on the back when things go well and acting as though you're the great I Am. Don't come on too strong or be too pleased with yourself, for you can be sure that pride comes before a fall, and you don't want to take a tumble, do you?

All your personal affairs should go with a swing now, and dealings with others will also be enjoyable and enlivening. Relationships will blossom and bloom, and you might even meet someone who brightens up your life and gives you a wonderfully new and exciting outlook on the world. In fact, that's just what you want, and you're eager to expand your experiences, increase your understanding and enrich your life in any way you can. You're especially anxious to turn your back on attitudes, ideas or habits that have hung over from your childhood and are holding you back from developing the inner you and making the most of your current circumstances and situation.

Your social set-up could go from strength to strength, but don't forget to do some exploring into the more serious and spiritual side of life. There's lots you could learn now about the whys and wherefores of the world, so dig deep to discover some of its secrets.

JUPITER IN YOUR SECOND HOUSE

Money, money, money! There's definitely a flavour of finance in the air, so stand by for a year when fiscal affairs are to the forefront of your thinking. It's a grand opportunity to put your money where your mouth is, or to invest your hard-earned cash in ways that will transform those pennies from acorns into mighty oaks of affluence. Even stashing away a little cash every month will give you the makings of a nice little nest egg, so why not investigate some simple savings schemes or insurance policies, or splash out on solid stocks and shares? Who knows, with expansive Jupiter behind you, you might even pick a real winner and end up much better off than you imagined! In fact, don't be surprised if a windfall or two lands in your lap now, for there could be a real bounty of boodle coming your way.

Whilst we're on the subject of money matters, this is also a grand time for making major purchases, especially if they'll grow in value over the years ahead. However, what you must guard against is buying something swanky or preposterously pricey just for the sake of it, or so you can keep up with the Joneses. Better ask yourself why you want something expensive (and answer honestly!) before forking out for it, then you're less likely to be lumbered with a luxury you don't really need or burdened by a big bill you can't afford to pay. Possessions you already own will also be important to you now, and you might even discover that something you thought was worthless is actually your passport to prosperity.

As Jupiter beams his way through your second solar house he's pinpointing all your values, both material and spiritual, so don't ignore the things in life that money can't buy. In fact, you might realise that those are the very things that mean the most to you, and change your life accordingly. This is a time when you'll discover there's much more to the world than meets the eye.

JUPITER IN YOUR THIRD HOUSE
Day-to-day dealings get a shot in the arm, now that genial Jupiter's watching over them. Maybe your everyday encounters become more rewarding and enriching, you meet someone who really takes you out of yourself, or the pace of your life perks up no end in all sorts of wonderful ways. A simple event could point you in an unexpected direction and start you off on a new interest, a neighbour may open up doors of opportunity and exploration that you'd never even dreamed of, or perhaps a community crusade or campaign develops from a pastime into something much more permanent?

Communications with others will also open up fresh horizons, so get talking to the folk you see every day and discover what really makes them tick. You're also much more open and honest than usual, for you want folk to know you as you really are. Whenever any problems arise you'll be able to discuss them with candour and clearsightedness, for you're not frightened of showing what you think and how you feel. In fact, this is your chance to clear the air if there's been a misunderstanding or mix-up because you'll be able to put your cards on the table and say what's on your mind. It's also a smashing time for being with close relatives, for not only will you enjoy their company but you'll also help each other in ways that could be financial or just plain friendly. Day trips or short visits will also be extra enjoyable and informative now, so start venturing away from home.

Whatever your usual prejudices and preoccupations, you're less likely to follow them at the moment. Instead, you want to judge things for yourself and are much more open-minded and objective about all aspects of life. Why not make the most of it by discovering new people or places, or learning more about the world? It could be the start of a fascinating voyage of mental exploration that you'll never want to end!

JUPITER IN YOUR FOURTH HOUSE

Home and hearth are of prime importance to you now, for you really need the peace, security and safety that they bring. In fact, it's a terrific time to concentrate on family matters, your home, your past and your inner sense of security, so let benevolent Jupiter be your guide to increasing your happiness at home.

Been thinking about investing in bricks and mortar by buying an abode of your own, or moving to somewhere that's bigger and better than your present pad? Then start talking to estate agents now, for this is a golden opportunity to make your money work for you and discover the dwelling of your dreams. If that's not on the cards or you're as happy as Larry in your current wee nook, then how about redecorating or expanding it in some way that will enhance its value and increase your comfort? Even if you just change the carpets and curtains you'll find extra enjoyment and happiness within your own four walls.

Being within the bosom of your family will mean a lot to you now, for it's the ideal time to put down roots. Arrange gatherings of the clan if they live far away, keep up with all your kith and kin and do anything else that will increase your sense of security and belonging. In fact, the more home-minded you are now, the more those warm feelings will stand you in good stead in the years to come, for you can establish ties and loyalties now that will never be broken.

Whatever problems come your way now you should turn to your family and close friends for support – and you'll gladly do the same if one of the clan is in need of help. Delving deep into your memories could also tide you over in times of trouble, perhaps by reminding you of a solution that has worked before, or reassuring you that you're not alone. This is a comfy, cosy and caring time, so make the most of it!

JUPITER IN YOUR FIFTH HOUSE

Razzle dazzle, that's you! Love, leisure and pleasure are on the way, so roll up your sleeves and prepare to enjoy yourself to the hilt! With the arrival of jubilant Jupiter, the planet of expansion and opportunity, in the solar abode of creativity, happiness and enjoyment, there's no doubt that you're all set for an interlude of frolics, fun and laughter.

One of the easiest aspects of this propitious period is that your self-expression is given a big boost. There's a super shine and sparkle to your personality, you're gregarious and generous, vital, vivacious and vibrant, and definitely the life and soul of every party you grace. What's more, you're blessed with a ravishing ring of confidence that helps you to stand out from the crowd and also improves all your relationships because you feel you've got nothing to hide from others. There's just one thing to watch – beware of being so sure of yourself that you swagger and strut about like Lord or Lady Muck!

When it comes to creative concerns, you're even more inspired and imaginative than usual now, so bring out your artistic aptitude in any way that takes your fancy. Doing what comes naturally will be easier than ever, but why not turn your hand to some new projects too? After all, you don't know what you can do till you try! If you want to make some extra cash, how about turning a hobby into a little money-spinner?

Affaires de coeur could also be on the astrological agenda now, whatever the current state of your heart. If you're a single soul, then you may not stay that way for long, and the chances are you could fall for someone from another clime or culture. Off on a trip to the sun? Then don't be surprised if a holiday romance develops into something much more serious. Wedding bells are definitely in the air, and news of a wee babe could also come your way. Enjoy yourself!

JUPITER IN YOUR SIXTH HOUSE

Work is on the astrological agenda now, and you're really in the mood for it. Whatever you do in your daily dealings, whether you're a director or worker, or you spend your days at home, you'll find your work fulfilling, satisfying and enjoyable whilst Jupiter's trundling through this solar sphere of your chart.

Promotion or extra responsibilities could come your way soon, but you'll happily tackle whatever task you're offered. If you want to change jobs, then now's the time to put in your applications, for you could be offered just the post or position you've been looking for. On the other hand, if you've been working away like a trooper without any recognition, this could be when your boss or employer finally notices all your sterling efforts. Even if there's no chance of promotion or a pay rise you'll still work to the best of your ability, for the sheer satisfaction of knowing that you've done your utmost. You'll also get on well with colleagues, clients, superiors and employees, and your bonhomie and good humour will oil the wheels of work at every opportunity. You're a super person to have around!

When it comes to health, you should be feeling bright-eyed, bushy tailed and generally on top of the world. If you've been under the weather lately, or are recovering from an ailment or illness, then you'll soon start to feel better. There's only one fly in the ointment, and that's your avoirdupois. Take care with the grub and grog if you find it easy to put on weight, for this could be when you really pile on the pounds if you're not careful. Remember that jocund Jupiter rules expansion, and that could easily apply to your waistline while he lingers in this astral abode! Take plenty of exercise, go easy on fattening foods and try not to overindulge your sweet tooth. That way, the only things that will expand will be your health and happiness, not your hips!

JUPITER IN YOUR SEVENTH HOUSE

Partnerships of all persuasions, whether platonic, professional or passionate, are all set to blossom and bloom, thanks to the positive presence of jolly Jupiter in your solar abode of one-to-one affairs. The folk you know could reveal new aspects of themselves that you'd never even imagined, and they may also bring out facets and factors in your own personality that have never seen the light of day before. In fact, this isn't a time to go it alone, so pal up with others wherever possible or you'll miss out all round!

If you're one half of a contented couple, then your relationship is about to get better and better, enriching and enlivening your life and increasing your pleasure, respect and faith in each other. Even if things have been less than loving lately, Jupiter's giving you the chance to make amends and get your affair back on an even keel, so make the most of this time of reconciliation and regrowth. In fact, all your dealings with others will be benevolent and beneficial, especially if you need to seek a chum's advice. Experts could be especially helpful, so don't bottle up your problems when you could share them with someone in the know.

The more you keep your mind and your options open, the more likely you are to encounter some fascinating folk. Maybe you'll meet someone from another country or a different way of life who expands the boundaries of your brain and increases your understanding of what makes folk tick? Who knows, you might even marry or settle down with an amour from another creed or culture. One thing's for sure, all your one-to-one affairs are suffused with a captivatingly cosmopolitan and fruitfully foreign flavour that will add a delightful dash of *je ne sais quoi* to all your encounters. Ooh la la!

JUPITER IN YOUR EIGHTH HOUSE

If money makes the world go round, then yours is all set to start spinning like a top, thanks to the advent of affluent Jupiter in your solar sphere of shared affairs. You're bound to benefit from someone else's generosity, whether it arrives in the form of an inheritance, insurance policy or tax rebate, or a wonderful wee windfall from a big-hearted buddy. On the other hand, if you're the one with all the boodle then you'll be happy to hand some of it over to folk who are trying to make ends meet.

It's a grand time to pool your resources with others, whether that means opening a joint bank account with all your savings or starting up a business or venture that makes the most of your combined talents and skills. One thing's for sure – you'll fare much better being part of a team than if you try to go it alone. Thinking of applying for a mortgage or a big loan from a bank or building society? Then you couldn't have picked a better time to ask, for fiscal favours are definitely coming your way now and money magnates will be more than eager to help you. Well, what are you waiting for?

Big changes in your life could also be on the way, especially if things seem to have been jogging along in the same old way for years on end. Now, don't worry – optimistic Jupiter brings golden opportunities, not dreadful disasters, so your life should take a richer and more rewarding turn and reveal new insights into your own personality as well as the characters of the folk around you. Have you been feeling worried, unhappy or dissatisfied with your lot lately? Then why not explore the more serious side of life by delving deep into philosophical and spiritual subjects? The truths you learn and the insights you gain could give you fresh hope and a new reason for living.

JUPITER IN YOUR NINTH HOUSE

Look, listen and learn! You're filled with a thirst for knowledge that knows no bounds now, so grab every opportunity to expand the horizons of your mind, increase your understanding of life and enrich your appreciation of the world around you. Join your local library, sign up for a few adult education classes or watch some serious television programmes and soak yourself in anything else that will provide you with plenty of food for thought. Don't just stick to the true, tried and tested, for this is a grand chance to discover different topics and add more strings to your bow. If there's a subject you've always wanted to study, then now's the time to tackle it!

Travel is also on the astrological agenda, for the world's your oyster now and it's offering you plenty of pearls of wisdom. How about embarking on the holiday of a lifetime and heading for a place you've always wanted to visit? Any trips will be enjoyable now, but they'll be best of all if you're willing to try pastures new, so act the explorer and set off on your own safari to one of the four corners of the world.

Your views, ideas and expectations are bound to change now, transforming your thinking and revealing fresh aspects of your personality. You might also meet folk who stimulate your mind and encourage you to abandon your preconceptions and prejudices so you can think things through for yourself and stop jumping to conclusions that have no foundation in fact. What a wise wee thing you are!

Environmental concerns or ecological campaigns could appeal to you too, and so will anything associated with religion, philosophy, politics or psychology. The more you learn now, the more you'll gain and the richer your life will become, so drink deep from the well of knowledge!

JUPITER IN YOUR TENTH HOUSE

The sky's the limit, so aim high! You're about to embark on a period when your professional potential, career capabilities, status, social success and reputation will get a big boost from expansive Jupiter, bringing acclaim, applause and achievement within your grasp. Even so, these things won't land in your lap unless you make a little effort too (you'll come unstuck if you expect Jupiter to do all the hard work whilst you sit back with your feet up!). Apply for new jobs, put in for promotion, ask for a pay rise and show superiors and bosses what an asset you are. There could also be the chance of going on business trips or dealing with folk from foreign lands, so be ready to pack your bags when the call comes.

There's just one thing to watch, and that's acting as though you've got all the answers and are the best thing since sliced bread. Beware of coming on too strong, being too big for your boots or letting your ego swell up like a barrage balloon, for that will simply make folk determined to trip you up or do you down. On the other hand, it might be you who has to deal with someone who's arrogant, overbearing, opinionated, bragging or boastful. If so, tread with care.

Ever wished you had more qualifications or even thought you should retrain for a completely different job or profession? Then why not seek expert advice and discover what you can do? Any extra skills or techniques you learn now will be added strings to your bow and could come in very handy in the future. If you want to stand out from the crowd, then this is your chance to tower head and shoulders above everyone else! Recognition and rewards are yours for the taking!

Parents, mentors and father figures could also play an important role in your life now, helping you when you need their advice, giving you their backing and letting you know they care. They'll form the solid support you need.

JUPITER IN YOUR ELEVENTH HOUSE

Whatever you want for the future, this is your chance to go after it whilst kind-hearted Jupiter casts his benevolent beams over your treasured hopes, wishes and dreams. This could be when you convert your castles in the air into reality, put precious plans into action or turn ambitions into achievements, so don't waste any opportunity to make your wishes come true! Remember, 'if only' are two of the saddest words in the English language, so banish them from your life by making a start at gaining your goals and reaching your objectives. Take one day at a time and you'll be astonished at the progress you make!

Friends are also important now, whether they help you to get what you want out of life or are just good company when you're relaxing. Social set-ups should be extra enjoyable (although they could also be extra expensive, so keep a close eye on your wallet!), and your circle of friends may expand when you meet exciting new folk as you get out and about. What's more, they could show they're worth their weight in gold in the future, and you'll return the compliment whenever it's needed. A friend might also introduce you to a once-in-a-lifetime opportunity and, if you're trying to make ends meet, a pal could come up with some much-needed cash just when you're wondering what to do.

The more people you're with at the moment the happier you'll be, so surround yourself with as many friends and acquaintances as possible and jump at every offer to get out and about. You could also become involved in activities or organisations with an idealistic or humanitarian aspect, when you realise that you want to help other people and improve their lives as well as your own. This is a time when you'll receive more than you give, whether it's good or bad.

JUPITER IN YOUR TWELFTH HOUSE

Life is about to take on a more serious and spiritual slant, when you'll want to explore your own identity, discover the hidden depths of your personality and mull over some of life's many mysteries. Even if you're usually wary of thinking too hard about the darker side of your personality or facing up to your fears, phobias, foibles and failings, you'll be able to look at them all fair and square now and begin to cope with them.

You're also able to put your ego on the back burner of life, so you can consider others first and yourself second. Charitable and altruistic activities will appeal now even if they usually leave you cold, so get involved in a local good cause in some way – you could find you enjoy it so much that you're still helping out long after Jupiter's moved off on his travels around the zodiac! If you already help folk who are less fortunate than yourself then your work will be even more satisfying and enjoyable than usual.

Are you trying to balance the budget or wondering how

to make the money go round? Then this is the time to ask about grants, bursaries and loans, for if you talk to an expert you could discover you're missing out on all sorts of entitlements and financial help you never even knew about. What's more, that helping hand could arrive just in the nick of time!

Someone you meet now, or whom you already know, may act as a mentor or spiritual teacher even if that isn't their usual role in life. Alternatively, you could be the one who's acting as a guide to someone in need, whether or not you're aware of it at the time. A thoughtful and transforming time.

SEEKING OUT THE SERIOUS SIDE
OF SATURN

Ever felt you're being held back by your own fears and phobias, or that folk don't really know the true you because although you seem bright and breezy on the surface you're a mass of insecurities and inhibitions inside? Well, that's all because of serious Saturn and the planetary position he occupies in your birth chart. Read on, and you'll uncover one of the most significant and sensitive sides to your personality.

The position of sturdy Saturn in your birth chart pinpoints your strengths and weaknesses, fears and self-confidence, ambitions and limitations, and shows how you deal with them. Saturn rules Capricorn and shares the rulership of Aquarius with Uranus, so he is a very important planet for people born under either of these two signs. In astrology, Saturn represented limitation and conservatism long before astronomers discovered that the planet really is limited itself by rings that appear to enclose it in a rigid framework.

THE SERIOUS SIDE OF SATURN

Usually the only way to discover Saturn's placing at the time of your birth is to consult an astrologer or look it up in a special book called an ephemeris, but I've made it easy for you by listing Saturn's movements through the heavens from 1900 to 1994. Saturn usually takes between 29½ and 30 years to complete his journey through the 12 signs of the zodiac although, as you'll see if you look at the chart plotting his progress, he sometimes moves out of one sign and goes back into the previous one for a short stay (which we astrologers call 'turning retrograde'), before going forward again (which we call 'turning direct').

If you look at the chart you'll see that, as well as giving the date and year when Saturn switches signs, I've also included the time (using the 24-hour clock). That's because you may have been born on a day when Saturn swops signs so, if you know the time you were born, you'll be able to discover which of those two signs applies to you. To use the chart, let's pretend you were born on 25 December 1943. Saturn didn't change signs on that day, so you have to look at the previous date – in this case, 8 May 1942. You'll see that Saturn moved into Gemini on that day, and didn't move out again until 20 June 1944, so Gemini is the sign he occupies on 25 December 1943. Now let's pretend you were born on 3 January 1962. If you look at the chart, you'll see that Saturn did change signs on that day, just after seven o'clock in the evening (19.01). If you were born at nine o'clock in the morning (09.00) Saturn would have been in the previous sign of Capricorn, but if you had been born at nine o'clock in the evening (21.00), Saturn would be in Aquarius, because he moved into that sign at 19.01. So what do you do if you've only got a vague idea of the time you were born, such as during the night or in the afternoon, but it was on a day when Saturn switched signs? Well, in that case your best bet is to read the descriptions of Saturn in both those signs, and then decide which one sounds most like you.

Now, before you get on with the important task of

working out which sign Saturn occupied at the time of your birth (why not look up the dates of your friends and family too?), there's something else about Saturn that's interesting to know. Because he takes roughly 30 years to complete a single circuit around the solar system, he will return to the sign he occupies in your birth chart when you are roughly 30, 60 and 90. Astrologers call this time the 'Saturn return', and say it is a time to reassess, restructure and rebuild your life. When looking back at their lives, many people realise they got married, changed careers, had babies or altered their lives in a very fundamental fashion when they were about 30, and go through similar changes (such as retiring from work or becoming grandparents) when they are 60. And if they're still going strong at 90, who knows what they'll do!

SEEK OUT SATURN'S POSITION IN YOUR BIRTH CHART

January 1900		Sagittarius
21 January 1900	08.10	Capricorn
18 July 1900	17.32	Sagittarius
17 October 1900	05.03	Capricorn
19 January 1903	22.17	Aquarius
13 April 1905	08.40	Pisces
17 August 1905	00.40	Aquarius
8 January 1906	12.48	Pisces
19 March 1908	14.23	Aries
17 May 1910	07.29	Taurus
14 December 1910	23.11	Aries
20 January 1911	09.19	Taurus
7 July 1912	06.12	Gemini
30 November 1912	18.19	Taurus
26 March 1913	13.06	Gemini
24 August 1914	17.28	Cancer

7 December 1914	06.48	Gemini
11 May 1915	21.23	Cancer
17 October 1916	15.35	Leo
7 December 1916	19.21	Cancer
24 June 1917	13.53	Leo
12 August 1919	13.52	Virgo
7 October 1921	17.23	Libra
20 December 1923	04.26	Scorpio
6 April 1924	08.34	Libra
13 September 1924	22.00	Scorpio
2 December 1926	22.34	Sagittarius
15 March 1929	13.48	Capricorn
5 May 1929	04.19	Sagittarius
30 November 1929	04.22	Capricorn
24 February 1932	02.47	Aquarius
13 August 1932	11.14	Capricorn
20 November 1932	02.09	Aquarius
14 February 1935	14.08	Pisces
25 April 1937	06.29	Aries
18 October 1937	03.40	Pisces
14 January 1938	10.32	Aries
6 July 1939	05.47	Taurus
22 September 1939	05.16	Aries
20 March 1940	09.41	Taurus
8 May 1942	19.40	Gemini
20 June 1944	07.48	Cancer
2 August 1946	14.42	Leo
19 September 1948	04.35	Virgo
3 April 1949	03.41	Leo
29 May 1949	12.56	Virgo
20 November 1950	15.48	Libra
7 March 1951	12.16	Virgo
13 August 1951	16.42	Libra
22 October 1953	15.35	Scorpio
12 January 1956	18.45	Sagittarius
14 May 1956	03.46	Scorpio

10 October 1956	15.11	Sagittarius
5 January 1959	13.32	Capricorn
3 January 1962	19.01	Aquarius
24 March 1964	04.17	Pisces
16 September 1964	21.04	Aquarius
16 December 1964	05.39	Pisces
3 March 1967	21.31	Aries
29 April 1969	22.22	Taurus
18 June 1971	16.08	Gemini
10 January 1972	03.44	Taurus
21 February 1972	14.51	Gemini
1 August 1973	22.20	Cancer
7 January 1974	20.27	Gemini
18 April 1974	22.33	Cancer
17 September 1975	04.56	Leo
14 January 1976	13.17	Cancer
5 June 1976	05.08	Leo
17 November 1977	02.42	Virgo
5 January 1978	00.45	Leo
26 July 1978	12.02	Virgo
21 September 1980	10.48	Libra
29 November 1982	10.28	Scorpio
6 May 1983	19.31	Libra
24 August 1983	11.52	Scorpio
17 November 1985	02.09	Sagittarius
13 February 1988	23.50	Capricorn
10 June 1988	05.23	Sagittarius
12 November 1988	09.25	Capricorn
6 February 1991	18.51	Aquarius
21 May 1993	04.58	Pisces
30 June 1993	08.29	Aquarius
28 January 1994	23.43	Pisces

SATURN IN ARIES

Oh dear! Do you ever feel you're being pulled in two completely different directions, wanting to be bold and accept challenges whilst inside you're quaking and quailing at the very thought? Or do you surprise yourself at the way you're assertive and aggressive sometimes and then indecisive and inhibited at others, even if you know you aren't acting in your own best interests? Well, it's all because the cautious and careful characteristics of strict Saturn are at odds with the eager and enthusiastic attitude of Aries, so no wonder you can feel confused by your perplexing personality! Never mind, for once you get used to this planetary paradox inside you, you'll be able to turn it to your advantage. Sturdy Saturn has imbued you with extra persistence and a dogged determination to succeed, especially when life looks like getting you down, so make the most of it and you'll be astonished at your own success and sense of self-worth. Your grit and gumption will stand you in super stead and will be extra useful if you were born with the Sun in Gemini, Libra or Pisces, which may make you tempted to give up when the going gets tough.

Take care whenever life hits a slack or boring patch, for that's when you could fall foul of depression, discontent, dreariness or a dreadful feeling of restlessness – your best bet is to work it off with some steady and regular exercise, but don't go overboard or you'll do yourself more harm than good!

SATURN IN TAURUS

How patient can you get? In your case, the answer is that you've got the stuff of a saint, and often put up with problems, struggles or setbacks that would leave lesser folk flummoxed and fed up. You're also cautious and careful to a considerable degree, but sometimes you take that to extremes and become so convinced you're right and everyone else is wrong that your strong-minded views turn into stubbornness (especially likely if your Sun sign is Taurus, Leo, Scorpio or Aquarius). Watch out!

Never mind, for you're kind and considerate, and this is a placing that brings ambition, achievement and acclaim, particularly when it comes to earning enough loot to be able to spend it on life's little luxuries. There's no doubt you enjoy the best that money can buy, but do you ever feel torn in two when out shopping? Is part of you saying 'Go on, spoil yourself' as you gaze at all the goodies on sale, whilst another part of you is saying 'Why not save your money instead? You don't really need that'? Sometimes that carping little voice will prevent you buying what turns out to be a pig in a poke, but don't let it rule your life and make you feel guilty even when you're buying some spuds or treating yourself to a bar of chocolate! A more serious danger, especially if you're naturally very shy and withdrawn, lies in changing from being a safe shopper who steers clear of impulse buys to one who's a wee bit more frugal – or even downright mean and mercenary!

SATURN IN GEMINI

What a brainbox! There's no doubt you've got what it takes when it comes to those little grey cells, for the cerebrally sensational combination of Saturn and Gemini has imbued you with a sharp mind, an objective attitude and clear thinking. You're also blessed with the ability to sum up a situation in a few words, and folk appreciate your wisdom and wit. On the other hand, they can dread getting the sharp edge of your tongue, for when you're hurt, angry or annoyed you can be sarcastic, cynical or sour (especially if you were born with the Sun in Gemini, Virgo or Capricorn). What folk don't realise is that you're usually hardest on yourself, and can be full of self-criticism when you think you've done something wrong. Just as you must learn to temper your criticism of other people, so you must learn to be kinder to yourself and not be so swift to highlight and dwell on your own faults and failings.

Instead, make the most of your super sense of humour by laughing at yourself and you'll find life becomes much easier to cope with.

Communications with others are often prone to misunderstandings and muddles with this placing because, although you may think you're being matter-of-fact and to the point, the folk on the receiving end think you're being brusque or that you're cross with them. What a muddle! Scientific subjects may appeal to you, for you've got the sort of cool analytical brain that can understand them, and you could also do well as a teacher. Make the most of your brain power!

SATURN IN CANCER

Emotional security is of paramount importance to anyone born with Saturn in the caring sign of Cancer, and if that's you then you'll do everything possible to ensure you feel safe, secure and happy. The trouble is, it's not always easy for you to express your emotions and let loved ones know just how much they matter to you, and your reserve and reluctance can sometimes lead to problems in partnerships. Maybe you should work out what you're afraid of, then decide whether it's realistic and rational or simply fears left over from your childhood that are still making you unhappy?

If your Sun sign is Cancer, Virgo, Capricorn or Pisces then your natural tendency to worry will be enhanced by this placing, so beware of letting yourself turn into a bag of nerves! Your greatest worries will concern kith and kin, ranging from fears for their welfare to anxious moments when you wonder if they really love you. Beware of staging scenes or indulging in emotional blackmail to get people's attention, for that will only work against you in the long run. Remember, the best way to get others to love you is just to be yourself, so calm down, stop feeling sorry for yourself and tell your dear ones how much you care. You're an ideal home-maker, and are probably extra clever when it comes to spotting bargains for your abode. You're also good at the day-to-day business of making the money go round and even putting some aside for a rainy day. What's your secret?

SATURN IN LEO

Leo is ruled by the Sun, and it's the most creative, out-going, happy and fun-loving of the 12 signs, yet when Saturn moves into Leo he casts a long shadow over all those terrific traits and dampens down the usual Leonine *joie-de-vivre*. Instead, anyone with this planetary placing will take life very seriously indeed (unless they also have the Sun in Aries, Leo or Sagittarius, which will help to cheer them up no end). If that's you, then you'll know that your strong sense of honour and deep determination to succeed are at the root of the problem – when you're working towards an objective you're so single-minded you won't let anything or anyone deter you from reaching your goal. Your organisational abilities are second to none, and you really come into your own when telling other people what to do (in the nicest possible way, of course!), controlling business dealings or overseeing the smooth running of the office or factory floor. Just make sure you don't think your job or occupation is the be-all and end-all of your existence, and you'll be fine.

Even if you've never been near any of the Forces, you can sometimes talk to yourself as though you were on the parade ground, issuing orders or placing such an over-whelming emphasis on duty and the idea of doing things because you have to that you make your life a misery. You've got to learn to relax and enjoy yourself more, and put life's problems into their proper perspective – you'll be astonished at the difference it makes!

SATURN IN VIRGO

What a worker! You dot all the i's and cross all the t's, determined to do as good a job as possible whether you're washing the car, cooking a meal or running a company, and your methodical nature rarely goes unnoticed (especially if you've got the Sun in Virgo or Capricorn). You're practical, pragmatic, patient, painstaking and prudent, but beware of adding pedantic to the list! Let's face it, sometimes you can be a wee bit too careful and cautious, or a stickler for convention even when there's a quicker and easier method of doing things. You're never going to be accused of cutting corners!

Even though you have such high standards, you must learn to be tolerant of lesser mortals who aren't blessed with your patience, dedication or ability, especially if you're the boss and they're the workers. Try not to carp at folk when they do something wrong, or wither them with a biting and searing sarcasm that does more harm than good in the long run. Remember, not everyone has your high standards, or is able to achieve them! However, your fault-finding doesn't just concentrate on other people, for you're also good at running yourself down and picking holes in your abilities. You hold your own actions up to your stringent scrutiny and often find them wanting, but you must learn to tread the fine line between trying to do better and expecting the impossible. What's more, you've got to beware of damaging your fragile self-confidence by running yourself down – come on, accentuate the positive and eliminate the negative!

SATURN IN LIBRA

Super! Your sense of fair play and strong belief in justice earn you many friends and stand you in superb stead whatever your daily doings. You've got a reasonable, rational, impartial and objective outlook on life and can usually strike the happy medium when it comes to making decisions or judgements. Even though folk born with the Sun in Libra are noted for their indecisiveness and inability to make up their minds, strong Saturn helps Libra in this particular placing, so if you've got the Sun, as well as Saturn, in Libra you should find it much easier to make decisions than other Librans. Kindness and consideration are your watchwords, so it's no wonder people enjoy being with you. You're also ace at being tactful and choosing your words carefully, making you an asset in any job or activity that calls for someone able to pour oil on troubled waters.

Partnerships of all persuasions are of prime importance to you, for you need to know you're loved and liked, and you get very hot and bothered whenever there's a rift in a relationship. If you've got the Sun in Aries, Cancer or Capricorn there may be times when you feel frustrated, fed up or just plain furious with partners for no apparent reason. Maybe you always find fault with colleagues at work, your family drive you to distraction or your other half often arouses your ire? Well, there are probably deep-seated reasons for your wrath that lie buried in the past, and digging down into your memories could uncover the root of the problem and ensure your future relationships are much more pleasant, positive and productive. Why not give it a go?

SATURN IN SCORPIO

Talk about still waters running deep! There's much more to you than meets the eye, and even if you've got the Sun in light-hearted Aries, Gemini or Sagittarius, folk will realise there's plenty going on behind your bright and breezy exterior. One of the characteristics that make you stand out from the crowd is your deep determination to succeed, whatever the cost and no matter how long it takes. You'll stick to your guns come what may, making the most of your reserves of energy and perseverance, but take care that your single-mindedness doesn't turn into bloody-mindedness, making you hell-bent on completing what you set out to do even if it would be better to call it a day or try another tack. Choosing the right job is of particular importance for you, because you need to find something that involves you one hundred per cent – if you aren't emotionally wrapped up in what you're doing then you'll feel dissatisfied, cheated and angry.

Your grit and doggedness are especially valuable when it comes to business dealings or money matters, and you could swiftly rise to the top of your tree. You're also good at handling shared affluent affairs, such as the family's finances, although sometimes you may indulge in extravagant urges and splurges that plunge your bank account firmly into the red. What you must watch out for are feelings of jealousy and envy (especially if you've got the Sun in Scorpio), which can slowly fester within you until they assume mammoth proportions and wreak havoc in your relationships. Don't let them get the upper hand!

SATURN IN SAGITTARIUS

Now here's a funny thing! As you probably know by now, Saturn represents restriction and holding back, but Jupiter (which is the planet that rules Sagittarius) signifies expansion and letting go. Sometimes that can cause problems, but often these contrasting planets will work hand in glove to produce some very positive personality traits indeed. For example, the concentration and care of Saturn will do wonders for that Sagittarian thirst for knowledge, enabling you to study hard, expand and enrich the frontiers of your mind and make the most of your brain power. You're also quite a philosopher at times – you were even when you were a child – and are probably interested in all sorts of serious-minded subjects.

Do you ever find your moods swing from one extreme to the other, leaving you walking on air about one thing but feeling down in the dumps about another? That's because Saturn is the sign of pessimism and Jupiter is the sign of optimism – put them together and it's no wonder your emotions go up and down like a yo-yo! Another possible pitfall is that part of you is raring to go and discover new people, places and pastimes, whilst the other half is reticent and retiring and would rather stick to the true, tried and tested. If you've got the Sun in Aries, Leo or Sagittarius you'll be much keener on venturing forth and living life to the full, but if the Sun was in Taurus, Virgo or Capricorn when you were born then you'll probably be wary of challenges and worried about sticking your neck out. Does that sound like you? Then bring out all the positive qualities of genial Jupiter and learn to live a little!

SATURN IN CAPRICORN

This is a very powerful placing indeed! In fact, it's a double dose of steadfast, stringent Saturn – he rules the sign of Capricorn and so his influence is very profound and pungent here. There's no doubt that there's a very serious side to your personality, although other placings in your birth chart will decide if you've got a lighter side or whether you're a right old Eeyore through and through! Even if you're usually quite cheerful and bright, Saturn's strong influence will still be there, making you cautious, determined, practical, pragmatic and ambitious. In fact, you're so concerned about having money in the bank (and keeping it there!) and the material security that boodle brings that you could easily turn into a workaholic, doing as much overtime as you can manage and bringing work home with you to boot. Don't fall into the Capricornian calamity (which will be extra likely if you've got the Sun in Virgo or Capricorn) of never seeing your family and friends, or working yourself into an early grave – no one's indispensable, you know!

If you're a parent, beware of coming on strong and acting in autocratic and dictatorial ways, because constant cricitism, fault-finding and nit-picking will do the kids more harm than good. Is it also the way you talk to yourself, always dredging up a list of misdeeds and wrongdoings, that undermines your self-confidence and makes you feel worried, wretched and worthless? Then stop being so hard on yourself, start concentrating on your good points and bring out your super Saturnine sense of humour to see the funny side of life. You've got a lot more to offer than you realise!

SATURN IN AQUARIUS

As with the previous placing, this is a very powerful position for steady Saturn because he shares the rulership of Aquarius with unruly Uranus, and that's where the trouble can start. Imagine the weird combination of the most conventional one of the twelve signs (Capricorn) with the most way-out and wacky (Aquarius), and you've got some idea of what this perplexing placing can be like! Very often you're torn between going out on a limb and being a true individual, or toeing the line and doing what's expected of you. If you were born with the Sun in Taurus, Virgo or Capricorn you'll probably bow to convention (even if you're cross with yourself for doing so), whereas if you've got the Sun in Aries, Gemini, Scorpio, Sagittarius or Aquarius you'll probably go your own way and raise eyebrows all round!

Folk may feel that they don't really know you, because you probably keep a small part of your personality locked away where no one can reach it. You're also very independent, though it could be in ways that surprise the people around you. That is even more likely if you've got an emotional Sun sign such as Cancer or Pisces, because you'll be affectionate and friendly in some ways but rather standoffish in others. Folk enjoy being near you because you're such an interesting, stimulating and surprising person, and they also like your positive and hopeful attitude towards the future. Keep up the good work!

SATURN IN PISCES

Supremely sensitive, self-sacrificing and sympathetic, that's you! In fact, you've probably got a heart of gold, and can be incredibly selfless and kind when the need arises, making you happy to help anyone in need. The milk of human kindness definitely runs through your veins but you'd be the last person to admit it, because you've got such a low opinion of yourself. Let's face it, you've probably read this far and decided it doesn't apply to you, even if you've just given someone the shirt off your back or donated some of your savings to a good cause! Standing up for yourself, speaking out or putting yourself forward are all difficult tasks for you, and sometimes you'll hold back even if it means losing out in some way or doing yourself down.

Beware of big black bouts of depression and woeful worry, especially if you were born with the Sun in Cancer, Virgo, Capricorn or Pisces, because they affect you very badly indeed. Try to work your way out of them by making the most of your innate creativity, especially if you can use your incredible imagination at the same time. You may not even realise how clever and inspired you are, so remember that creativity comes in many forms and isn't just about painting pictures or playing the piano. Cooking, gardening or just appreciating other people's hard work all come under that heading, so do what comes naturally and enjoy the sense of satisfaction that will steal over you. Go on, spoil yourself for once!

RUSSELL'S SUN SIGN GUIDE TO FAMOUS FOLK

ARIES

Joan Crawford	23 March 1908
Steve McQueen	24 March 1930
Diana Ross	26 March 1944
John Major	29 March 1943
Doris Day	3 April 1924
Eddie Murphy	3 April 1951
Bette Davis	5 April 1908
Severiano Ballesteros	9 April 1957
Charlie Chaplin	16 April 1889
Clare Francis	17 April 1946

TAURUS

HM The Queen	21 April 1926
Jack Nicholson	22 April 1937
Shirley MacLaine	24 April 1934
Ella Fitzgerald	25 April 1918
Audrey Hepburn	4 May 1929
Michael Palin	5 May 1943
Fred Astaire	10 May 1899
Stevie Wonder	13 May 1950
Pope John Paul II	18 May 1920
Cher	20 May 1945

GEMINI

Joan Collins	23 May 1936
Queen Victoria	24 May 1819
Clint Eastwood	31 May 1930
Marilyn Monroe	1 June 1926
Raoul Dufy	3 June 1877
Prince	7 June 1958
Cole Porter	9 June 1891
Judy Garland	10 June 1922
Beryl Reid	17 June 1920
Errol Flynn	20 June 1909

CANCER

Meryl Streep	22 June 1949
Esther Rantzen	22 June 1940
Henry VIII	28 June 1491
HRH The Princess of Wales	1 July 1961
Tom Cruise	3 July 1962
Louis Armstrong	4 July 1900
David Hockney	9 July 1937
Harrison Ford	13 July 1942
Nelson Mandela	18 July 1918
Diana Rigg	20 July 1938

LEO

Mick Jagger	26 July 1943
Jackie Onassis	28 July 1929
Benito Mussolini	29 July 1883
Yves St Laurent	1 August 1936
HM The Queen Mother	4 August 1900
Lucille Ball	6 August 1911
Madonna	16 August 1958
Mae West	17 August 1892
Robert Redford	18 August 1937
Bill Clinton	19 August 1946

VIRGO

Sean Connery	25 August 1930
Mother Teresa	27 August 1910
Michael Jackson	29 August 1958
Pauline Collins	3 September 1940
John Smith	13 September 1938
Agatha Christie	15 September 1890
Lauren Bacall	16 September 1924
Greta Garbo	18 September 1905
Sophia Loren	20 September 1934
Bruce Springsteen	23 September 1949

LIBRA

Felicity Kendal	25 September 1946
Michael Douglas	25 September 1944
George Gershwin	26 September 1898
Brigitte Bardot	28 September 1934
Julie Andrews	1 October 1935
Mahatma Gandhi	2 October 1869
Lady Thatcher	13 October 1925
Roger Moore	14 October 1927
Ralph Lauren	14 October 1939
Martina Navratilova	18 October 1956

SCORPIO

Pablo Picasso	25 October 1881
John Cleese	27 October 1939
Cleo Laine	28 October 1927
Roseanne Barr	3 November 1953
Richard Burton	10 November 1925
HRH The Prince of Wales	14 November 1948
Rock Hudson	17 November 1925
Jodie Foster	19 November 1962
Goldie Hawn	21 November 1945
Jamie Lee Curtis	22 November 1958

SAGITTARIUS

Tina Turner	25 November 1941
Jimi Hendrix	27 November 1942
Sir Winston Churchill	30 November 1874
Woody Allen	1 December 1935
Maria Callas	2 December 1923
Dame Judi Dench	9 December 1934
Ludwig van Beethoven	17 December 1770
Keith Richards	18 December 1943
Jenny Agutter	20 December 1952
Jane Fonda	21 December 1937

CAPRICORN

Maggie Smith	28 December 1934
Marlene Dietrich	27 December 1901
Sir Anthony Hopkins	31 December 1937
Joan of Arc	6 January 1412
Mel Gibson	6 January 1956
David Bowie	8 January 1947
Faye Dunaway	14 January 1941
Dr Martin Luther King	15 January 1929
Dolly Parton	19 January 1946
Stefan Edberg	19 January 1966

AQUARIUS

John Hurt	22 January 1940
Oprah Winfrey	29 January 1954
Germaine Greer	29 January 1939
Vanessa Redgrave	30 January 1937
Boris Yeltsin	1 February 1931
Me!	5 February 1952
Charles Dickens	7 February 1812
Mia Farrow	9 February 1945
John McEnroe	16 February 1959
Julia McKenzie	17 February 1942

PISCES

Jilly Cooper	21 February 1937
Julie Walters	22 February 1950
Elizabeth Taylor	27 February 1932
David Niven	1 March 1909
Mikhail Gorbachev	2 March 1931
Frankie Howerd	6 March 1922
Liza Minnelli	12 March 1946
Michael Caine	14 March 1933
Nat King Cole	17 March 1919
Glenn Close	19 March 1947

THE TRADITIONS OF ASTROLOGY

SIGN	NOs	COLOUR	STONE	DAY	METAL	FLOWER	BODY AREA
Aries	1	Red	Diamond	Tuesday	Iron	Geranium	Head
Taurus	2	Copper, dark blue	Emerald	Friday	Copper	Daisy	Throat
Gemini	3	Yellows	Agate, garnet	Wednesday	Mercury	Daffodil	Hands, chest
Cancer	4	Pearl, silver	Pearl	Monday	Silver	White rose, lily	Breast
Leo	5	Amber, gold	Ruby	Sunday	Gold	Sunflower	Heart, spine
Virgo	6	Autumnal shades	Peridot	Wednesday	Mercury	Lily of the valley	Intestines
Libra	7	Pastel blues and pinks	Sapphire	Friday	Copper	Rose	Kidneys
Scorpio	8	Black, burgundy	Opal	Tuesday	Iron	Dahlia, rhododendron	Sexual organs
Sagittarius	9	Imperial purple	Topaz	Thursday	Tin	Delphinium	Thighs, hips
Capricorn	10, 1	Black, grey, white	Turquoise	Saturday	Lead	Pansy	Shins, knees
Aquarius	11, 2	Turquoise, blues	Amethyst	Saturday	Lead	Crocus, snowdrop	Ankles
Pisces	12, 3	Greens, sea blues	Aquamarine	Thursday	Tin	Poppy	Feet

WHAT 1994 HAS IN STORE
FOR YOUR
LOVE, CASH AND WORK

LOVE

It's said that the path of true love never runs smooth, yet for amorous Capricorns, 1994 will be a time of sweet sentiment and avowals of affection. The year begins with you in a passionate and forceful mood, and you can be sure that the months to come will have their fair share of challenges which you can easily overcome with the help and support of those who love you! With the mighty vibes of Mars, Venus and Mercury making hay in your sign in January, the prospects for the year are stunning in all areas, affairs of the heart included. Of course when Uranus and Neptune go their wayward course through your sign from May to October, you'll tend to feel insecure and unsure of yourself, so the comforting presence of your kin and loved ones is extra important to renew your confidence. Take care from 12 June to 3 July, for when mini Mercury takes a brief detour in your horoscopic house of partnerships your usually taciturn tongue takes on a sharp note and misunderstandings can too easily occur from ill thought-out words. This is the only fly in the ointment as far as your emotional security is concerned in 1994. Your deeply passionate and often well-concealed amorous nature is superbly stirred right through the year with high points of intimate intensity in the April–May period and during July and August! A disagreement amongst your friends could cause complications in October, but it's time some grievances were aired. It's better out than in, Capricorn, and you'll find that straight talking will eventually sort out any problems in your social set!

CASH

We all know how important the subject of the bank balance is to all self-respecting Capricorns, so it's a relief to know that there aren't any serious pecuniary problems in store in 1994. You should be able to increase your hoard without too much bother. That's not to say that there aren't any hiccups, though, for when Mercury backs up in a retrograde course into your solar house of finance and worth in late February, even the most canny Capricorn could be persuaded to part with some of the hard-earned! The trouble is that purchases and investments made at this time will turn out to be nothing but trouble. You usually don't have any problem keeping a hold on the pennies, so clutch the purse strings just a little tighter until you get the celestial all clear on 19 March!

One of the best financial indicators of the year is Saturn's long-awaited move out of your finances house at the end of January. This means that the tough days are nearly over, and you can safely loosen your belt as the dark days of your personal recession fade into memory.

The end of 1994 should be a particularly profitable time, for mighty Mars manoeuvres through a web of red tape concerning contracts, agreements, insurance policies and investments ensuring a comfortable financial future. You're such a canny soul!

WORK

It's likely to be an action-packed and exciting annum for you, Capricorn! Ambitious and hard working as you are, you'll have no problems in dealing with the professional challenges that are set to occur throughout 1994. The early part of the year runs as smooth as silk even though you'll be feeling a little vulnerable after May and in need of reassurance of your worth and future. The wayward wanderings of Mercury, Uranus and Neptune make you extra sensitive to changes of mood and subtle undercurrents in the workplace, which does nothing for the steady Capricornian sense of ordered progress! Late October too shows a period of some professional concern, but all will be put to rights by the 30th when Mercury sees the merit of the slow but sure path to success and sets your feet on the road to career advancement!

YOUR DAY-BY-DAY GUIDE TO 1994

JANUARY

SATURDAY, 1st. Can this be a new Capricorn this New Year's Day? Does your list of resolutions include flinging caution to the winds? Well, if this is a new start for you at least you're endowed with a super-abundance of self-assertive energy and want to shine like the superstar you really are! Anyone who tries to make you take second place could regret their actions as they feel the full force of your formidable temper. Sweep away any obstacle to your full self-expression, whether it's a meek manner that no longer becomes you or a partner who doesn't realise the full power of your personality. You're likely to be such a dynamic daredevil right through 1994!

SUNDAY, 2nd. Confidence failing you just a mite, Capricorn? All those wild and wacky resolutions of yesterday seem so far away now as the sobering influence of your planetary ruler Saturn gets together with the atomic rays of Pluto. In fact you could get the idea that some of your friends are taking you for a ride just now, stretching your good nature to the limit. If so, then confront them with your opinions at once and air your views rather than let a martyr complex develop.

MONDAY, 3rd. After yesterday's sombre sky, Mars is goading jolly old Jupiter in the heavens and the result is a highly enjoyable start to the week, even more so if you are the sort of Goat that wants company and is ready to explore new horizons. If not, then try to put this burst of creative energy to some use.

TUESDAY, 4th. You've really found your feet now, for you speak with authority on every subject you tackle, and the densest of folk can't help but take notice of your

pronouncements. If you have important business arrange-
ments or interviews to see to, this is the perfect day, for
you'll impress everyone you meet with your articulate eloquence and self-assured fluency with words and ideas.

WEDNESDAY, 5th. Your life resembles riding a roller-
coaster just now, because every good day you get is bal-
anced out with one that's fraught with insecurity and stress.
This Wednesday your ego's on the ropes and getting a bit of
a battering, but there's no need to throw in the towel.
You'll feel deflated and demoralised until you find a new
direction that you can channel your energies and talents
into. Try not to let minor setbacks get you down!

THURSDAY, 6th. You see, every down day *is* followed by
an uplift! This time your personality is power-charged with
charm as macho Mars rubs shoulders with Venus, the lady
of love. That should boost the old prestige. If you've got a
favour to ask, do it now while Mars gives you all the
confidence and drive you'll ever need, and Venus pumps up
the charisma to bursting point. With such a potent duo on
your side I don't think you'll be refused!

FRIDAY, 7th. The mechanics of your life seem to be in
good working order, so if you want to get moving on any
personal projects or lay the plans for a future wish, then do
so now. You have an awesome power which, if directed
singularly without any diversions or distractions, can make
you the success you deserve to be. A day when you can
really find your feet.

SATURDAY, 8th. Emotionally you're in an intensely sensitive mood as you get an inkling that you're on the brink of
something profoundly important in your life, though
you're not quite sure what it is yet. Take yourself off for a

stroll away from the beaten track, or a quiet spot where you won't be disturbed, as you can't abide an interruption when you're so deeply immersed in thought.

SUNDAY, 9th. It's a good thing today's not a workday, for you're not at your shrewdest or sharpest. In fact, not to put too fine a point on it, you're apt to be taken for a ride by anyone with dishonest intent, for you're mentally muddled and muffled by an oversensitive desire to believe the best of everyone. It's an admirably charitable approach, but it'll leave you defenceless against unscrupulous folk, so don't agree to anything you might regret later.

MONDAY, 10th. It seems you'll have to put in a good day's work and make sure your affairs are in order before you even think about any larking around this Monday! It sounds dull to any empty-headed folk who come your way but what do they know about the solid satisfaction of knowing you've done your duty? A very pleasant day for all canny Capricorns, for once your chores are done you'll really enjoy a spot of social celebration!

TUESDAY, 11th. Maybe it's a delayed reaction from the prodigious partying you've been doing over the past Yuletide season, but whatever the cause you'll be feeling weak, wan and weary this Tuesday. Your usual down-to-earth outlook is confused and clouded by an influx of insight, inspiration and intuition. Follow a hunch and you won't go far wrong, but don't expect to tackle anything too arduous or exacting.

WEDNESDAY, 12th. An idealistic impulse has you in its grip Wednesday, attuning you to the true meaning of charity and caring, and encouraging you to play your part in promoting peace on Earth. Speak up about your personal vision, however unrealistic or airy-fairy it may seem, as people will comprehend the kindness, consideration and compassion behind your words. Idealism inspires you now.

THURSDAY, 13th. An erratic Uranian outburst is triggered off by the Sun in your most personal world now, overturning any old-fashioned ideas and inviting a more contemporary identity. Try some trendy togs and a total turnaround in your image, as these will serve to improve and enhance your future prospects. Head into the unknown – you can cope with the challenge!

FRIDAY, 14th. Commercial and business plans will take off positively this month if you put yourself in the picture and don't rely on information from others. Stocks, shares, bonds – indeed, all sorts of monetary investments – look profitable if you consult the experts and find out what's really happening on the financial fronts. This is a fabulously productive period as that mini mastermind Mercury gets to grips with the financial realities of your life.

SATURDAY, 15th. The Sun's golden rays are gloriously gilded and garnished by voluptuous Venusian vibes Thursday, enveloping you in an appealing and attractive aura that'll have the whole world waiting eagerly to adore you! If you're on the lookout for love you have the seductive allure required to capture the heart of someone special now, whilst financially you also stand to profit.

SUNDAY, 16th. You're so lovely these days! A velvety Venusian aura fills your sign with an attractive and alluring ray that's increased and enhanced Sunday by the Sun's sensational presence. If you're in any way unhappy with your appearance this is the perfect time to give your whole image a facelift, for your taste is without equal now. Don't be surprised if you find folk flocking around just to catch a sight of you, for you're oozing charm and charisma from every pore!

MONDAY, 17th. This is an excellent day on which to travel. If you want to negotiate or put forward plans or ideas then do so now. Funnily enough, without appearing to pressurise people around you, you actually get your way quite a lot now, as you come across as being so nice that folk don't want to hurt or offend you.

THURSDAY, 18th. While your eyes are fixed so firmly on the far future horizon Tuesday, you should take the opportunity to think your ideals and aspirations through in detail, as there's no point in sticking to a plan of action that no longer suits your true inner ambitions. A gradual transformation has been pushing you in another direction, and you should eliminate any connections or convictions that are standing in your way. A little constructive ruthlessness is called for.

WEDNESDAY, 19th. Your aura is enhanced with a gorgeous glow of opulent luxury as Venus glides into your solar home of valuables and boodle, imbuing you with a taste for the very best that life has to offer. Let your nearest and dearest have a few hints about the kind of beautiful things you've been hankering after, and perhaps you'd like to get yourself a little something just to keep you going. Nothing but the best is good enough for your refined preferences.

THURSDAY, 20th. There's still an opulent glow to your stars as the heavens' most gracious and majestic body, the Sun, moves his mighty presence into your solar house of money to join lucky Venus from Thursday. This could prove to be a most affluent period for you, so don't rest on your financial laurels. Instead, take this opportunity to lay some nest eggs or to sort out economic plans for future security and stability.

FRIDAY, 21st. An uneasy suspicion that you're in the process of pulling the rug out from under your own feet in a personal matter will put you right off your stroke today. But remember it doesn't really matter if you do step away from all that's known and familiar, as you'll soon weave yourself another rug of beliefs and convictions to stand on. An adventurous spirit will take you boldly forward and you won't regret a moment of it.

SATURDAY, 22nd. You're not the most romantic sign of the zodiac dozen, and quite honestly I can't see much sentiment sloshing around your stars today no matter how amorous your other half is! You're far more interested in simply getting on with the usual round of activities than in making some romantic gesture guaranteed to win the heart of your love. Make a fuss of your loved one, as you've been so busy these days that they may be feeling neglected.

SUNDAY, 23rd. 'Oh, the expense!' I can hear you groan as you take a peek into your wallet and find nothing but a huge gaping hole. If you're wise you'll cast your mind back to all the fun and frolics you've been enjoying and realise that money truly isn't everything. You may have to break into your emergency funds to end this week, but your long-term prospects are splendid, so why worry?

MONDAY, 24th. The richest rewards in this life often come purely on merit, and from the hard work you've been putting in lately you're clearly due for a spot of applause, adulation and appreciation! If the praise comes in the form of hard cash or a prospective boost in your income, then so much the better! If your health hasn't been too good don't hesitate to invest some money in medical advice, a proposed cure or a treatment not available through the NHS.

TUESDAY, 25th. Friends, neighbours, relatives – today you should spend some time with someone or another. There is a feeling of happiness in the air so join a club or whist drive, or perhaps have a drink at a bar on the way home. What you mustn't do is play the martyr, complaining that nobody loves you and the world couldn't care less. Do something about it, for heaven's sake – get out and about and make an effort to be sociable.

WEDNESDAY, 26th. A sharp rebuke from your other half or your own crusty conscience rousing you to action makes Wednesday a very active, alert and exhausting day. The trouble is, you're so busy bustling about yourself you just can't stand to see anyone pulling less than their full weight, and that could lead to a few unpleasant altercations if you're not careful. Remember, not everyone has your get-up-and-go these days, and if they want to squander their lives in idleness, that's their problem!

THURSDAY, 27th. Yet again you knock 'em dead Thursday with your powerfully sexy personality, radiating desire to everyone you meet. Who can resist your seductive charms or the potent individuality that makes you the person everyone wants to be with? If you don't feel the *femme fatale* or Casanova type just now, give it time and you could surprise yourself!

FRIDAY, 28th. Your natural Capricornian reserve is highlighted now as the taskmaster of the heavens, your ruler Saturn, brings weight to bear on your solar house of correspondence and communications. You're entering a serious-minded patch when your ideas and opinions must be reviewed, whilst any pitfalls lie in letting sombre thoughts turn to depression and despondency. Be confident.

SATURDAY, 29th. Warlike Mars marched into your horoscope's house of wealth and worth yesterday. Economic failings or doubts affecting your self-esteem can no longer be tolerated under his energetic influence, so set about boosting your boodle. Your self-confidence will benefit from an improvement in your economic standing, and the solution to past problems lies in your own hands. Maybe you could insist on a more affluent income from your employers, or embark on an enterprise designed to produce considerable profits.

SUNDAY, 30th. Yesterday you dazzled 'em with your drive and ambition, and today you can bring the big guns of your pure charm and debonair diplomacy to bear. Financially you'll be on to a winner, as whatever you do you can count on some influential support from on high. Take the trouble to acknowledge any help with your sweetest smile and most affectionate thanks and you'll be all set for a secure and happy future.

MONDAY, 31st. Professionally you'll be super-sensitive to any hints or rumours about your position and your prospects, but for once this isn't a source of anxiety and worry as all that you hear is good and encouraging news! A word with the boss, or with folk in authority, could do your economic situation the world of good, especially if you take the trouble to point out just how far your excellent abilities are liable to take you!

FEBRUARY

TUESDAY, 1st. You're a real live wire from Tuesday as communications speed up and you're in the mood for meeting, chatting and mingling with people from all walks of life. It's an excellent time to arrange appointments, apply for positions or enter into detailed negotiations. You'll hear from a brother, sister or other close relative and a short journey will offer ample opportunity for making new contacts.

WEDNESDAY, 2nd. If you've been neglecting your pals you'd do well to put in an appearance at your regular meeting place, as it always makes sense to keep in touch. While you're at it, why not give your social life a boost and arrange a soiree or bash for all your buddies to enjoy? You enjoy being in the thick of things, and need to swing out a bit when parties are on the menu.

THURSDAY, 3rd. If ever there was a day to be self-reliant this is it! With such a tense connection between the Sun and Jupiter the whole world seems to be off doing its own thing. If you were expecting a friend to pay back a loan or help you out on a money-making venture then think again, for Thursday at least. Your best bet is to carry on as best you can and take all promises with a pinch of salt, especially if they are to do with money. You remember the old one about the cheque being in the post . . . well!

FRIDAY, 4th. If I were you I'd think at least twice before you open your mouth at all this Friday! Mother Moon's emotional influence dims the clear light of logic and reason, making you far more susceptible to irrational and imaginative impulses than you realise. Don't kid yourself that you're being totally reasonable in all you say, for quite frankly you're in a proper mental muddle today!

SATURDAY, 5th. No one can avoid facing the fact that Saturday shopping sprees can turn out to be expensive, so take care if you do plan to wander round the shops looking for bargains. You're apt to let a touch of panic buying take over and that could cost you dear in the long run as you realise you've parted with your cash for unsuitable or shoddy items. Don't let anyone persuade you to part with any cash unless you are absolutely sure that you'll get value for money.

SUNDAY, 6th. With your diligent and dutiful nature you need to make sure you get a proper break from the hustle and bustle of the workaday world, for you give of your best and must expect to take some time for recharging your batteries. Whatever strikes you as the most restful occupation, from inspecting your estate to pandering to a sweet tooth with an array of delicacies, should be indulged in now – after all, this is supposed to be a day of rest!

MONDAY, 7th. Take a personal problem to a pal renowned for their wisdom, and sure enough you'll receive some excellent advice and a spot of cheerful encouragement thrown in for good measure! There could be an innocent ulterior motive as they ask for your support in return for a cause they feel is just. So long as you agree, it's an opportunity not to be missed.

TUESDAY, 8th. Uranus has been stirring things up in your own sign for some time now, but you never quite get used to the idea that a certain amount of change in your personal life can be a very good thing. That's your problem today, for although you can see the sense of updating your image, whether through a modern outfit or a more fetching hairdo, you can't help trying to cling on to the old ways. Let go of the past, Capricorn, for the future awaits!

WEDNESDAY, 9th. Someone you perceive as a threat to your financial security could come in for some very sharp criticism Wednesday as you lash out in a devastating defensive reflex. If they're really out to cheat you, your aggressive response is justified, but are you positive you're not taking too seriously a gesture meant in jest? Your temper's a touch too explosive for your own good at the moment.

THURSDAY, 10th. Everything that you hold as precious and valuable in life must be put under a ruthless review now, for there's a New Moon in your horoscopic house of wealth and worth signalling the start of a brand-new era. Do your personal possessions really represent your true tastes? Are your finances geared up to take full advantage of modern fiscal developments? These are the searching questions you must answer for yourself now.

FRIDAY, 11th. I hope you've been vigilant in returning phone calls and answering letters, as Friday sees the beginning of a perplexing period where communications are concerned. Messages will tend to go adrift and journeys could lead you into detours and delays that bring you grinding to a halt in the next few weeks. With extra care and caution you can keep the wheels turning, but it'll take dedication.

SATURDAY, 12th. You can charm the birdies clean off the tree with your silver tongue, Capricorn! If you've got a case to put forward or a conversation to have with folk who are normally difficult to win over, fret no more, for you can alight on winning words and punctuate your dialogue with such beautiful phrases that you'll be able to get your way with any philistines in your midst.

SUNDAY, 13th. By the pricking of your thumbs you know that something's up, for no one can hide anything from your perceptive eyes this Sunday. You'll amaze folk with your apparent ability to know what they're thinking almost before they've opened their mouths, and that'll encourage them to confide in you as you seem so sympathetic and understanding. Prepare to play the role of agony aunt!

MONDAY, 14th. Not the most romantic of the zodiac dozen, are you, Capricorn? I'm afraid that the romantic vibes of Valentine's Day pass you by as there are some practical considerations to be seen to before you indulge yourself in amorous pursuits. It's plain to you that there are urgent repairs and much-needed improvements required to bring your abode up to scratch, but your kith and kin have been dragging their feet over the expense involved. You know full well it would be a false economy to delay any longer, so take matters into your own hands, even if it means dipping into your own private contingency funds. It'll be money well spent and once your family see the improvements they'll soon reimburse you for your trouble.

TUESDAY, 15th. A pal who whisks you off for a spot of shopping this Tuesday should be treated with caution, as their infectious enthusiasm for certain expensive items could so easily tempt you into breaking your personal bank. Stick to a carefully prepared budget and lash out on luxuries you know for a fact you can afford. And I thought you were the one with the reputation of being careful with the pennies! I don't know what the world is coming to!

WEDNESDAY, 16th. How's the old abode looking these days? A little shabby around the edges, or untidy in certain chaotic corners? Roll up your sleeves and set to with a will, as any time and effort invested in making your residence as desirable as possible will reap rich rewards in terms of peace of mind and comfort. Don't be too busy to get some well-deserved rest in, though, for otherwise you'll overload yourself with stress again!

THURSDAY, 17th. You're convinced there's a dishonest pal in your midst who's trying to pull a fast one financially, but try as you might you can't get any cast-iron evidence. You're tempted to play the super-sleuth and track down some indication of their guilt, but aren't you getting a wee bit obsessed about the whole affair? It's much better to air your suspicions openly rather than carry on a guerilla war.

FRIDAY, 18th. Community affairs are close to the hearts of many Capricorns, whether it's the street you live in or, on a broader level, the town or county you belong to that's concerning you. Over the next weeks spend some time suggesting ways of making your locality a place to be proud of: write letters to people who can help, drum up support for a local issue and get involved in neighbourhood schemes.

SATURDAY, 19th. The zodiac's strict taskmaster, Saturn, has madcap Mercury under control Saturday and for you that means a day of disciplined and difficult thinking when you must work out a consistent and constructive position on some practical matters. It's a fine time to talk to folk who can advise you on your next step professionally, but only if you frame your queries concisely and clearly.

SUNDAY, 20th. It's not often I can call you a chatterbox, but that's the only word for your garrulous and gregarious behaviour Sunday. You're fairly bubbling over with brilliant ideas on every topic under the sun, and can't wait to share your notions with folk who'll be impressed by your intellectual and expressive excellence! This is a fantastic day to follow up contacts with folk who could help you achieve a cherished ambition, for you'll quickly win them round with your verbal virtuosity!

MONDAY, 21st. From this evening you should begin to turn your attention to the fiscal facts affecting your goals. Mercury's slipped into your solar house of cash concerns, helping you to understand the economic implications of your actions. It's a promising period to apply for loans, ask for a raise or discuss pensions, savings and insurance matters.

TUESDAY, 22nd. Are you fully rested, restored and refreshed? I hope so, for your Tuesday stars demand your full attention as you come to a stage in your life when decisions must be made regarding your entire sense of direction. Think long and hard about what you want to achieve and maybe make a few methodical notes, for there's no room for mental muddle now. Talk to anyone else concerned about the practical implications of your ambitions, for they'll give you sound advice that should be heeded!

WEDNESDAY, 23rd. There's a tense and tricky situation developing in your material world that won't be easily settled unless you get off your high horse and agree to some frank and free-ranging discussions. There are some others involved who are just as stubborn as you, but it won't hurt to make the first move in order to unlock this stalemate. Avoid the temptation to act out of spite.

THURSDAY, 24th. A quarrel over joint finances will hardly start the day off with a swing. The trouble is, someone is taking liberties with your possessions or money and an ownership quibble could leave you complaining endlessly about the cheek of some people. It's important to keep calm and voice your grievances clearly. Quarrelling will cause resentment on both sides, and bottling up your negative thoughts will only cause internal stress. Be firm and as clear as crystal when you complain!

FRIDAY, 25th. You're normally so decisive and definite, but under Friday's confusing sky you're just not sure what it is that you *do* think. Opinions you thought were as unchangeable as the Rock of Ages seem to be wavering, and this can make you feel most insecure. Your mental world is going through a profound reorganisation and you'll need to accept some changes.

SATURDAY, 26th. Study and education should be uppermost in your mind, even if it's not your own you're concerned about. You're very astute mentally now and realise that you must gain more knowledge and broaden your prospects in many areas of your life. If you've been working toward extra qualifications, diplomas or exams, then all will come to fruition now.

SUNDAY, 27th. The cold days of February seem endless at the moment and thoughts of carefree travel to hot, sunny climes seem very attractive now. If you are already indulging in a wee winter break, or just contemplating the possibility, you should seize the chance to sample some unusual and exotic delights as you need to broaden your horizons and introduce yourself to new ways of thinking and being. Take a detour from the official guided trek and see how ordinary folk live – you'll be pleasantly surprised.

MONDAY, 28th. The Monday-morning blues hold no fears for you, Capricorn. In fact, you're hot on the trail of pleasure and profit, motivated by the masterly mingling of Mercury and Mars in your solar house of wealth and worth. Your mind's working with supersonic speed and decisive determination, sorting out ways and means of making a fast buck and ensuring long-term prosperity at the same time. If you're shopping for gifts and self-indulgent treats, avoid a hasty choice that may cost you more than you really need to spend!

MARCH

TUESDAY, 1st. When the atomic vibes of ponderous Pluto take a backward step, Capricorns will wonder where everyone's gone. For now at least you could be on a desert island for all the company that's around. It's true that the next couple of months will see various old companions and friends disappearing from your life for a while, but that gap in your social diary will be filled by new and interesting faces. So don't worry if you feel somewhat lonely Tuesday; the important thing is to keep yourself occupied during the lull. You'll soon see that old friends will turn up again, while new friends await to enrich your life.

WEDNESDAY, 2nd. Instead of simply toeing the company line you should act on your own initiative, especially where there's a chance to increase profits, as your ability to think for yourself will be greatly admired and appreciated. Whilst you're feeling so brave and bold, maybe it's high time you put in for a raise for some well-deserved promotion. It may seem a cheek, but you could strike it rich!

THURSDAY, 3rd. The only time that Capricorns can really get aggressive is when your personal security is threatened. This morning sees you in a fine fury but you'll eventually take pity on some of the bewildered recipients of your verbal blasts, and set about smoothing down any ruffled feathers. When it comes to gracious gallantry and cordial courtesy you'd make the most accomplished diplomat look positively clumsy this afternoon and can expect to restore the peace in record time. Make harmony your aim and you'll succeed beyond your sweetest dreams this Thursday.

FRIDAY, 4th. So far this week you've been dealing with some pretty important issues, so the heavens on Friday urge you to let your hair down and give fun and frolics a look-in! Your sociable impulse may be due to an unexpected invitation landing on your mat this morning, or someone you bump into quite by chance who's keen to catch up on old times. Make a break with your usual daily routine – it'll cheer you up no end!

SATURDAY, 5th. At last! News concerning a raise, tracing lost funds or allowing for your next monetary move should finally arrive, bringing an end to a stalemate that's cost you a pretty penny. Apply your brilliant brain to the task of setting a budget or finding out precisely where you stand financially, for mastermind Mercury's sharpened your mind to a piercing pecuniary point.

SUNDAY, 6th. Never one to miss an opportunity, you can really feel exceptional today. Never mind that it's not a workday – you really can't let a chance like this slip! Your future hopes and wishes receive an injection of solid celestial fuel today, as does anything requiring a lot of thought. Remember, it is your inborn geniality that makes you a winner today.

MONDAY, 7th. Business letters or important calls should be made this Monday. Contact the council, official departments or any other authoritarian person while the going's good, as you're in a self-assertive mood that can cut through the most tangled red tape. Take advice when necessary and avoid the temptation to override any local bye-laws and regulations.

TUESDAY, 8th. If you're thinking of decorating or have other designs on the home, then Venus will help you spread a hue of happiness over and around your abode. This couldn't be a better time to hang or drape sumptuous fabrics, curtains or cushions around your dwelling; choose blues, pinks and pastel shades that bring out the peace and harmony.

WEDNESDAY, 9th. A delightfully harmonious and satisfying day as the magical rays of the Moon smile sweetly on the generosity of Jupiter. A pet project will receive an injection of help from friends who are only too pleased to lend a hand this Wednesday. Your usually carefully concealed charms show through a crusty exterior, winning approval from all around you. Friends and colleagues are keen to assist you in any way that they can today. You can be such a charismatic creature!

THURSDAY, 10th. Some of the purchases you've recently made will occupy your full attention now as you go about fitting them in and generally arranging your home to make it as lovely and luxurious as possible. You certainly have fabulous taste these days, so don't be surprised if you receive a steady stream of admiring visitors picking up tips and asking advice. How very gratifying!

FRIDAY, 11th. An outing with friends is on the cards now, be it a coach trip from a club you belong to or a suggestion that one or two of you go on an away-day – anything that will get you out of the same old routine will be money well spent. Forget the day-to-day grind, forget onerous duties for once. I know Capricorns are hard-working achievers, but now's the time to playfully gambol like a kid again. Head for the hills, my friends!

SATURDAY, 12th. Your immediate environment and neighbourhood are what matter to you now. You could join in with a crusade about local issues, chivvy your councillor or MP, or decide that your town needs cleaning up socially or morally. Get on your soap box either by writing or talking to those in power, but make sure your voice is heard over and above the rabble.

SUNDAY, 13th. Those down-to-earth considerations that have been eluding your mental grasp finally become concrete and within your comprehension today. You may feel that you're up against it and on your own against the odds, but you need to sort out your ideas in the light of common sense and in a spirit of balance before you get the support and understanding that's due. Loved ones may seem mercenary, but they're really only being practical and sensible.

MONDAY, 14th. Once your thoughts stray into an idealistic realm there's just no holding you these days as intuitive, instinctive and irrational ideas flood into your bedazzled brain. You comprehend the true meaning and value of qualities such as compassion and kindness, and should be prepared to include them to a much greater degree in your overall outlook on life. An item of news reaching you through the grapevine will bring a satisfied smile to your lips.

TUESDAY, 15th. You've been working hard and long on developing an idea that could improve and enhance your local community, only to meet with a cold refusal today from the powers that be. If they thought that would be the end of the matter they're very much mistaken, for once you've taken up a fight you'll do or die, Capricorn. Before you commit yourself to a course of confrontation, reflect on the benefits at stake and make sure it's really worth all the effort.

WEDNESDAY, 16th. Pillar of the establishment you may be, but unadventurous sheep you're not, for a mischievous spirit moves you today to come out with some unconventional opinions just to keep the people in your neighbourhood guessing about your true beliefs and ideals. It's quite clear to you that whilst some traditions must be preserved at all costs, there are other customs that should be abolished forthwith, and you're not afraid to say so either. What a controversial Capricorn!

THURSDAY, 17th. A most difficult situation brewing in your material world cannot be resolved, as you don't have any control over what's happening. You'll just have to sit back and wait for others to make decisions that affect your financial future, as there's little point in trying to apply pressure. You'll win through in the end, thanks to family aid.

FRIDAY, 18th. Whatever you'd assumed were your objectives in life, you should think things through from first principles now, and be prepared to ditch a few ideas that you've outgrown along the way. A bare acquaintance could come up with an idealistic idea that has a profound impact on your own opinions and aspirations. Now you know what you're aiming at, your world may never be the same again!

SATURDAY, 19th. This is a quite superb weekend for you if you are travelling, studying, writing or indeed putting some elbow grease into any ideas you have had for future plans. This is all due to the arrival of stimulating Mercury into your solar house of communications yesterday, increasing your sensational supply of intelligence, inquisitiveness, and eloquence. In the coming weeks you're in a cerebral class of your own!

SUNDAY, 20th. Any material plans will soon come to fruition if you lay some firm foundations over the next few weeks. You may decide to save your money, buy something that will serve as an investment or find a way of earning a few pounds more; whatever the case you should know exactly what you're aiming at. A major period for domestic renewal and happy families begins.

MONDAY, 21st. A little straight talking never hurt anyone, they say, and this time it's true, as a heart-to-heart with your spouse or partner clears the air and gives you both plenty of reason to put on a happy face. Whisk a loved one off to the bright lights and lap up some culture, as you deserve a taste of the good life. A busy and buoyant Monday, full of fun.

TUESDAY, 22nd. Your other half will be in a fearful and fretful mood as he or she notices the changes you're going through and can't help but wonder how things will stand between you in the future. Possibly you're not too sure yourself, which is small comfort to either of you, but honesty is your best policy. Any attempt to evade the issue and pretend that nothing's wrong will only add to your problems.

WEDNESDAY, 23rd. Others make a song and dance about all material possessions these days, but tasteless boasting and senseless show is just not your style. Instead there's a secret smile on your lips that betokens a happy heart filled with romantic rapture and private passion! A tiny token from someone you know is sincere means so much more than huge flamboyant gestures of casual affection.

THURSDAY, 24th. What tremendous Thursday stars! The go-ahead galactic scene packs a very positive punch and in your world it's through constructive contacts with others you'll find the opportunities awaiting. A friend could come up with just the job opening you've been looking for, or a neighbour's contacts overseas may bring you a chance to act on an objective you've long held. It's very much up to you to make the first move, but once you're in action plenty of astral energy is yours! Be a bold Goat now!

FRIDAY, 25th. It may be the end of the working week for some but yesterday's message has obviously gotten through to you as your mind is firmly focused on the demands of duty and obligation. It's a splendid day for making lists, organising rotas and plotting travel plans, as you're in the mood to get down to brass tacks and won't tolerate sloppy thinking or airy-fairy ideas. You're a practical paragon and folk will thank you for it!

SATURDAY, 26th. No matter what anyone says to you Saturday they'll come across as aggressive and sarcastic to your jaded and jittery ear, for you're convinced there are folk out to disprove your pet theories and discredit you in the process. This kind of touchy paranoia won't make you any friends, so try to curb your caustic tongue, however stupid and slow-witted some folk are. We can't all have an intelligence as acute as yours!

SUNDAY, 27th. Careerwise you're at a turning point, for unless you get back on course you could wind up in a dead-end that won't get you anywhere. Whether you're a high-flier professionally or aiming at more modest personal goals, now's your chance to review your strategy and make any adjustments needed to achieve maximum success and status. Some unexpected news could help you clarify your thoughts on the subject.

MONDAY, 28th. You shouldn't do anything too tiring or tedious as your stars foretell of a Monday filled with love and laughter. Invite the family round (only those you adore, of course!) or bake a few cakes and arrange an impromptu evening with a friend or two. If you've got to work, then make sure you do just those bits you enjoy and ignore the rest!

TUESDAY, 29th. A word in the ear of a friend could bear interesting fruit as you get wind of some group plans that are in line with your own aspirations and hopes. If you've been wondering how to find a practical way of expressing your idealistic vision for a perfect world, you'll find that you have partners who can help solve some of the stickier problems along the way.

WEDNESDAY, 30th. Usually taciturn Capricorns aren't exactly shrinking violets Wednesday. In fact you'll be talking nineteen to the dozen, bending the ear of anyone and everyone who will listen to your views. At least you can be sure that your opinions will be well thought out and rational, because when mastermind Mercury gets in gregarious mood with jolly Jupiter, fine conversations and fun encounters are to be expected. It's about time you loosened your tongue and shared your deep insights with others – of course, one or two laughs along the way will make it even easier for you to make your point.

THURSDAY, 31st. It's an enormous effort Thursday simply to get out of bed, let alone force yourself to leave the comfort of your abode and venture out into the wide world. As a diligent and dutiful soul you will if you must, of course, but just as soon as you can you should scuttle back to your glowing hearth and the comfort of carpet slippers, fond family and your softest armchair. Bliss!

APRIL

FRIDAY, 1st. A glorious Good Friday for enjoying yourself with fun-loving friends or folk who share your social interests. It's the beginning of a beautifully creative period that'll do your love life a power of good as voluptuous Venus vaults gracefully into the part of your horoscope concerned with affairs of the heart. Romance is in the air, and even sensible Goats fall prey to its sensational scent! Ah, it's true that love doth make fools of us all, but who'd have it any other way?

SATURDAY, 2nd. Along with your friends you've been fascinated by the mysteries of this world and want to do all you can to probe beneath the surface to a deeper understanding. Your perception is piercing, and intuitively you can lead the way to the heart of a mystery that's puzzled you for some time. Frivolous concerns leave you cold now, as your mind is firmly fixed on ideas and thoughts that can be taken seriously and treated with all due respect.

SUNDAY, 3rd. What a mental marvel you are today, Capricorn! As the Mercurial vibes get together with those of masterful Mars, the speed of your thought processes is simply breathtaking. It's true that you are usually quick on the uptake, but Sunday your grasp of even the most obscure points is awesome. Besides your brainpower and brilliance, you've also got an uncontrollable urge to communicate your insights to anyone who will listen – and since your eloquence is also boosted, that means anyone who happens to be to hand!

MONDAY, 4th. A luscious love affair that's enraptured you recently could be costing you an arm and a leg as you shower your loved one with generous gifts and tasty treats. I'm sure there's no need to be quite so extravagant, as they'll easily understand that your funds are limited, so let your head overrule your heart on this occasion and give your bank balance a breathing space!

TUESDAY, 5th. You may have to contact the DSS or a voluntary welfare organisation this Tuesday. If you're not directly involved with either, a selfless attitude and the determination to do something to help people will be uppermost in your mind as you see just how much need there is around you. Once your duty is done you'll enjoy an artistic hobby to soothe you.

WEDNESDAY, 6th. You're tempted to discuss your personal secrets far too openly as an energetic and emotional sky opens up your heart. If you have the urge to discuss your intimate business, make sure you don't betray a confidence and hurt someone dear to you. Constructive communications concerning mundane matters are a source of quiet satisfaction to you now.

THURSDAY, 7th. Well, my fine four-footed friends, it seems to me you've earned a bit of a break, so make the most of your tremendous Thursday stars. There's plenty of planetary peace coming your way in the form of helpful neighbours, a benevolent friend or sweet-natured youngsters ready to do your bidding. So stretch out, make sure there's a nice cup of tea on the way, and prepare to hold a very congenial court!

FRIDAY, 8th. Toss a few ideas around with your friends Friday and you'll be amazed at just how much can be revealed to you. You're fascinated by a mystery you're absolutely determined to get to the bottom of. With the help of some perceptive pals you'll be able to reach an excellent understanding of the deeper levels of your future aspirations, and forge a bond that comes from sharing the same ideals.

SATURDAY, 9th. If it's a while since you and your family sat down for a good chinwag, that situation could soon change for the better as mellifluous Mercury moves into your solar house of hearth and home, imbuing you all with an eloquence and wit that will bring your abode to life with the chatter of happy voices. Take the opportunity to discuss any matters, from the most serious to the most trivial, and you'll all feel much closer as a result.

SUNDAY, 10th. I know you're attached to your reliable and responsible reputation, but this weekend it wouldn't do you any harm to throw caution to the wind, as you're in an adventurous mood and need to sample some excitement. Surprise trips, or visits from folk fresh to your neighbourhood, all combine to show you a new and unusual world. Get moving, Capricorn!

MONDAY, 11th. Monday's forthright sky will spur you on to speak your mind, for you can see there are some important issues to be aired. Social reform strikes you as urgently needed and the chance may come for you to take the lead. Think things through and examine your own aspirations, for you have the skill to understand any complex problem in depth.

TUESDAY, 12th. Though Capricorns like to show a cool, self-assured exterior, there's a strong streak of pulsating passion bubbling away beneath the surface as the magical rays of Mother Moon meet the voluptuous vibes of Venus. There's more than a hint of romance in today's starry agenda, so put boring, mundane duties where they belong, in the background of your life, and prepare to let astral amour inject some pep into the workaday world!

WEDNESDAY, 13th. Unpack your paint brushes, dig out your knitting needles or polish up your penny whistle, for every aspect of the arts fascinates you now. Relax from the demands of your working world by letting your imagination run riot. But before you submerge yourself in a sea of fantasy, tune in to the emotional tones of a love affair and ensure you're not ignoring or overlooking someone else's feelings. Magic!

THURSDAY, 14th. Mars marches moodily into your solar house of the hearth and home Thursday, putting you in an argumentative and aggressive state. Channel your antagonism into some home decorating, DIY work or anything that requires strength, as domestic exertion will make the most of your vim, verve and vigour. Don't rile your relatives during this pugnacious planetary pattern.

FRIDAY, 15th. Are you sure you haven't been a shade too generous with the cooking sherry? I ask because your entire family appears to be wandering around in a fog this Friday. You're not too clear-headed yourself, so don't take any worrying news you may hear to heart, for the chances are the story's merely apocryphal. Watch out for your plumbing, for domestic waterworks could prove problematical.

SATURDAY, 16th. A little home cooking, the pleasure of your family's company and oodles of domestic security all combine to make you a forthright and confident Goat when it comes to pushing yourself to the front of any queue in your working world. Unemployed Capricorns should listen to some advice from the clan, as they know just where you should be headed and will pull out all the stops to make you contented in work matters.

SUNDAY, 17th. What a contrary and contradictory bunch your family is! First they moan about you being an old stick-in-the-mud, and then they complain that your ideas for bringing your abode up to date are far too wild, weird and way out! It does seem very ungrateful when you've been trying your utmost to cultivate a more modern image, but perhaps you have gone just a wee bit too far? Why not try a compromise between customary ways and your novel notions? At least that way you'll be able to live in peace!

MONDAY, 18th. Partnership affairs of all kinds, from platonic friendships to the most passionate liaison, need to be treated with a certain amount of tact if you're not to trample over some highly sensitive toes and blunder into issues that are best left alone. If you keep your eyes peeled for signs of distress, and then diplomatically change the subject, you'll be thanked with a loving gratitude that will make your forbearance worthwhile.

TUESDAY, 19th. A quiet word with a family member who appears tense or troubled will be very gratefully received today. Even if it seems a bit of an intrusion to tackle a topic you know is very sensitive, you should speak up and give them a chance to get a few of their fears and anxieties off their chest. It's a terrific Tuesday for healing a family rift, and communication is the crucial key.

WEDNESDAY, 20th. Right up until the end of May you have an opportunity to show your creative prowess and unleash your true potential as a unique individual. Concentrate on that thing that means more to you than anything else, for the time has come when you can obtain your heart's desire, and the more adventurous and enterprising you are the better. Use your skills and talents to the full.

THURSDAY, 21st. How long is it since you let your hair down, got dressed up to the nines and really enjoyed yourself? Well, even if it was last night you should seize any opportunity this Thursday to put your best sociable foot forward and prepare to be entertained, amused and enchanted! Paint the town a delicate shade of pink with your beloved, take an enthusiastic child out on an excursion or arrange to meet your pals at your local pub or club. You're in sparkling form!

FRIDAY, 22nd. Roll up, roll up! It's the first day of the rest of your life and you really don't want to miss any bandwagon that happens to be rolling along! An energetic sky blows a refreshing breeze through every corner of your world, and wakes you up to the fact that fame and fortune are within your grasp if you just get yourself up and going. Pursue your ambitions with drive and determination, and you'll really set your career ball rolling.

SATURDAY, 23rd. Though this is the start of the weekend, for you it's not a case of sitting back and letting career matters slide. In fact it's quite the opposite. You are in an inspired mood, Capricorn, and are ready to take advantage of any and all opportunities that come your way. It's going to be a day of turn and turn about as the unconventional rays of Uranus in your sign set you off on a course that will lead to great success. There is no obstacle you can't get over with ease now, as you're such a whirlwind Goat ready to scale the dizzy heights of ambition.

SUNDAY, 24th. An explosive array of temperamental planets greets you this Sunday and before long you'll be at loggerheads with your family or a close friend about something or other. The particular point is almost irrelevant as the real issue boils down to a question of authority. You and your antagonist are both determined to have the last say! Maybe you should just agree to disagree and leave it at that, for you're in an incredibly intransigent state of mind today.

MONDAY, 25th. You've been so busy conversing with the folk closest to you during the past weeks that you have neglected to make your position on many matters of importance clear to the world at large. Mischievous Mercury trots into your solar house of fun and games and ushers in a period of pranks and practical jokes that will fill your world with laughter and at the same time give you the opportunity to express your thoughts and opinions in a way that's unmistakable to all.

TUESDAY, 26th. Your entire working world is about to be blessed by the beautiful and bountiful presence of velvet Venus. Advancement in your employment will come through female colleagues in particular, and an office romance may be in the air. If you're looking for work, a vocation with an artistic element will be right up your occupational alley! Any lapse of self-discipline in the coming weeks will quickly have its effect on your physical fitness, so steer clear of too much grub and keep up a healthful attitude.

WEDNESDAY, 27th. By sticking diligently and doggedly to your guns today you should eventually get your message through. It drives you wild when folk put endless official objections and ridiculous red tape in your way, and you could be tempted to either give up in disgust or start ranting and raving at their unhelpful attitude. Neither approach will get you anywhere, so try to let off steam in some harmless way whilst never losing sight of your ultimate goal. A difficulty can be turned to your advantage simply by a display of your famous obstinacy and common sense.

THURSDAY, 28th. A generous friend could well point the way to the achievement of a long-held wish Thursday. Make a point of making time for a chat with comrades and companions. Even an idle word or joke could spark your mind off in a totally unexpected direction. Friends and those who hold you in high esteem are determined to aid you in your course in the world, so don't be a stick-in-the-mud Capricorn, tied down to your usual round of mundane duties – take a break! You could learn something to your advantage.

FRIDAY, 29th. Put the cares of the world to one side now that you're satisfied you've set some powerful wheels into motion, and spend some time talking things over with friends and family. Take the opportunity to let them know just how you feel, as it's not often you feel you can reveal your emotions, and it's an opportunity not to be missed.

SATURDAY, 30th. As you begin to have second thoughts about certain alterations you've made in your image in the hope of keeping up with the times, you'll be made to see that traditional ways and established ideas still have plenty to offer. Don't turn your back on this modern world, but do keep your feet firmly on the ground. The age-old values of reliability, common sense and canny caution will stand you in very good stead today.

MAY

SUNDAY, 1st. Children and teenagers are uppermost in your mind this merry May Day. If you've been having trouble with them, or perhaps if they've been involved with the wrong side of the law, you'll have some success in getting them back on to the straight and narrow now. A second chance is always worth giving, and you could do with the same treatment from a loved one yourself.

MONDAY, 2nd. If you're a working Goat you should thank your lucky stars for such kind, caring and comforting colleagues. It's the little things in life that make such a difference, like a cheery smile when you arrive in the morning and a good-humoured joke to help pass the time, and you shouldn't let them go unnoticed and unacknowledged. Let your workmates know how much you enjoy their convivial company. If you're jobless, a woman with a soft heart may be able to help.

TUESDAY, 3rd. You've achieved an income that's a pleasing source of security, but just out of sight there could be a fly lurking in the ointment in the form of a friend or acquaintance with ulterior motives. Any advice or information that's a bit secretive or confidential should be treated with a certain amount of suspicion, as there must be a reason for the secrecy, even if it's not at all obvious. Take care.

WEDNESDAY, 4th. You have a fine way about you this Wednesday, so much so that other folk will see you as a pillar of society, very generous and a hoot to be with. You are more chatty than usual and have the chance to express your feelings and opinions without upsetting anyone.

THURSDAY, 5th. It seems someone you thought you could trust may have been spreading some pretty unsavoury rumours around and the result is a crisis of confidence amongst colleagues and employers. As well as damaging your reputation, the gossip could hit you quite hard in the pocket as benefits you'd expected fail to come through. It'll take a while to set the record straight, so be patient.

FRIDAY, 6th. Friday dawns with a sweetly sentimental aura that puts you in mind of your most noble ideals and aspirations for this world. It's a perfect opportunity to have a chat with a concerned youngster about an ideological issue that interests them, for together you can unravel some of the mysteries of life, the universe and everything! Mentally you're inspired with intuitive insights now.

SATURDAY, 7th. The unpredictable planet Uranus in your sign has been playing havoc with the well-ordered pattern of your life for some time now, but today his whole influence goes into overdrive. In many ways this is a totally revolutionary day. Out with the old and in with the new! At last you will feel that you are embarking on a whole new and exciting chapter in your existence. Many of your fondest hopes and wishes are set to be realised, but only if you have the courage to pass through the doorway of opportunity that beckons. Be brave, Capricorn!

SUNDAY, 8th. A youngster you know has got hold of some weird and wonderful ideas from somewhere and it seems nothing you can say will persuade them of the error of their ways. The more you insist on setting them right the more stubborn they'll be about sticking to their guns, so try a subtler approach. A lovers' tiff could lead to some wounding words that will be difficult to forgive.

MONDAY, 9th. Frank discussion and fresh dialogue should be opened up businesswise. If you're dissatisfied in any way with your treatment, conditions or overall well-being in the workplace, now's the time to put your complaints in writing or to ask a senior member of staff or your shop steward to put your case. Appointments of a medical nature should also be made now.

TUESDAY, 10th. Pets, playthings and infants take centre stage in your world Tuesday, as the solar eclipse grants an astral opportunity to open a new creative chapter in your life. Maybe you're contemplating a new addition to your family, or feel it's time you developed your personal potential? Lonesome Goats could be on the verge of a fresh romantic beginning, too. Whatever your area of interest, you've every reason to feel bright-eyed and bushy-tailed!

WEDNESDAY, 11th. Summertime sun is more often than not a soggy affair here in Britain but today you're in red-hot form and ready to set the world alight with your bright ideas and brilliant charisma! You'll be personality plus this Wednesday as you decide to make a go of this attempt at a British summer and light up the lives of those around you with your brightest smile and cheeriest visage. You're such a little ray of sunshine!

THURSDAY, 12th. Workplace worries melt away in the first light of dawn as Thursday's stars usher in an era of peace and harmony between you and any cantankerous colleagues who've been rocking the boat. A dab of diplomatic perfume in all the right spots will soothe any ruffled professional feathers and make you all feel 100 per cent better as a result. Don't put up with strife when you can so easily turn it to sweet harmony.

129

FRIDAY, 13th. Forget the ominous omens of the date, because some dramatic developments in your domestic world that could bring so much fortune to boost your emotional security are in the spotlight, and you could find that they'll be rubbing off on your working world as well. Look for ways of bringing your own private good luck along to help a colleague or working partner, as you're always happiest when you're sharing and giving your selfless side a chance.

SATURDAY, 14th. You seem to be in a wan state of weariness and worry as your vitality and energy are drained by an awkward Mars–Neptune angle. Even if you're as fit as a fiddle, someone in the family could be ailing with a mysterious malaise that's throwing your plans off the rails. Don't assume the worst, for you're not thinking clearly now and may overdramatise the facts out of all proportion.

SUNDAY, 15th. You are now able to paint a new, more colourful picture on your canvas of life. The delectable refining ray bringing together the golden Sun with misty Neptune will enrapture your heart and fill your world with romance. Let's not forget the sensationally selfless you that emerges from the mist, giving your all to social and charity work for the good of others.

MONDAY, 16th. A merry jest or practical joke intended to bring a smile to those close to you could misfire if you're not very careful, for folk around now seem to have lost their sense of humour entirely. It'll be hard work at times today trying to get any point across, let alone raising a smile, so you might as well abandon it as a bad job. Your kith and kin are much more receptive to your sparkling wit and amusing anecdotes.

TUESDAY, 17th. As the Sun shines his majestic light full on your solar house of love affairs and creativity, you're inspired by an intuitive idea that comes to you from out of the blue and could point you in an entirely new creative direction. Perhaps news of a pregnancy will turn your world upside down, or an unexpected amorous encounter could open your eyes wide. The more flexible you are the better, as there's a new spirit in the air with much to offer you.

WEDNESDAY, 18th. If you're an incurable romantic (and there aren't many of us left!) and have a few little amorous secrets you don't wish to impart to your friends, you'll have a field day under Wednesday's super-secretive sky. Any furtive love affairs will flourish, as will any amorous needs you don't wish to reveal to the public eye. It's a profoundly fascinating and rather erotic day behind locked doors!

THURSDAY, 19th. There's trouble brewing in t'family! All it takes is a tiny incident for you to be confronting a domestic riot of mammoth proportions, and it's all down to a clash of egos between you and folk who think they know how to run your life for you. Maybe it *is* time you made your own way, but an angry departure will only leave a bitter taste. Keep your cool.

FRIDAY, 20th. There may be a dull outlook to the last working day of the week but you're in a far from dreary mood as your good humour puts a twinkle in your eye and a cheery grin on your face. You're a real pleasure to have around as you bring a ray of sunshine into the gloomiest situation, and it all stems from your wise decision today to look firmly on the bright side of life. What a winner you are, Capricorn!

SATURDAY, 21st. From now until late June you're in a creative class of your own! Sensational Sunlight streams into your horoscopic house of leisure and pleasure, producing a flood of fun-filled ideas and pleasurable plans. Whether you're playing the leading role in an amateur-dramatics show, putting pen to paper for your first novel or dabbling in the visual arts, you've the terrific talents required to make a scintillating splash! The pattering of tiny feet could bring joy to many Capricornian hearts this month.

SUNDAY, 22nd. Books, articles and leaflets about an academic subject that intrigues you capture your attention today and make this a Sunday when you're immersed in the exploration of ideas. Mentally you're as bright as a button, and want to add to your store of knowledge, especially if there's a chance it can help you to proceed to the top of the professional ladder!

MONDAY, 23rd. With a sigh of relief you'll find yourself being gently carried along by your usual Monday routine, for today's tender stars demand nothing more from you than easy-going acceptance. Socially you're in for an especially delightful day as friends flock to your side simply to pass the time of day as pleasantly as possible. Whilst everyone's feeling so affectionate, why not take a wee gift home to your other half to let them know how much you care? They'll be thrilled to bits!

TUESDAY, 24th. Mighty Mars made a very opportune entrance into your solar house of fun and frolics late last night, for he's just in time to inject a little punch and pzazz into your life. If you've been patiently waiting for romance to knock at your door, you'll suddenly realise that it's up to you to go out and hunt down the love of your life. With your divine looks, vigour and vitality it won't be long before you've swept someone special right off their feet!

WEDNESDAY, 25th. There are people and situations draining you emotionally dry. You may be soldiering on with feeble funds and skimpy support but you're gradually being worn to a thread to no purpose. If there is someone who won't help themselves or who tends to rely totally on you, ask for state help and find a way to be true to yourself, for whatever happens you must live your own life to the full.

THURSDAY, 26th. There's no mistaking it, Thursday is going to be a fabulous day for affairs of the heart for all coy Capricorns. Take the love of your life gently by the hand and do something fanciful and free like sweeping your beau or belle off their feet and treating them to some slap-up nosh. A candlelit supper in a select restaurant, complete with soft music and an atmosphere of amour, will put back some of the magic to your relationship. Lavishing some loving care and attention on that special person wil put a spring in both your steps!

FRIDAY, 27th. If you feel it's time to put a spot of scintillating sparkle back into a close relationship then this is your chance, now the feminine celestial contingent hold sway over your stars. Even if you've no wish to tangle with amour, you should reach out to the folk around and express your feelings, affection and gratitude to others. Go on, have a heart, and make this a super-special weekend for all!

SATURDAY, 28th. The emphasis on relationships continues today, so seize the chance proffered by Mercury today to discuss things further. There may be matters of great importance to talk about, but don't neglect the little things, for by chatting about everything from the price of fish to the progress of personal plans you're bound to renew the bonds of affection.

SUNDAY, 29th. Settle down with your bank statements or count the contents of your purse, for you need to feel that your economic world is shipshape and secure. Whilst you're in such an organised state of mind why not tackle a few odd jobs around the house by fixing up some broken or shabby possessions? Stick to the practicalities and it'll be a Sunday well spent.

MONDAY, 30th. You're convinced that you're plagued with an economic black hole that's been draining cash from your account in some mysterious way. You hate to feel out of control so you'll do your utmost to get to the bottom of the matter. Your detective work will pay off, as nothing can withstand a Capricorn's determined persistence, but there's no need to push your luck once you've settled the matter.

TUESDAY, 31st. After a time of complex changes as you try to inject a new spirit of excitement into your close associations, Venus steps in to take the sting out of any troubles and strife you may have been having. Acquiesce and compromise now over any upsets, prepare to forgive and forget and the future will look rosier, happier and much more contented.

JUNE

WEDNESDAY, 1st. A pal with a very big mouth will come up with a wizard wheeze aimed at making a mint out of a tiny investment and you're just optimistic enough to fall for it. Leaving it all up to luck like this is a sure way to squander your stake! If you've the sense to keep your activities within certain sensible limits, today's effervescent, exuberant and exhilarating sky can help you to accomplish fantastic feats of unsurpassed enjoyment. Socially you're in fizzing form!

THURSDAY, 2nd. What a poor old soul you are Thursday as you receive the full effect of the perplexed planets jostling for position in your own sign. It's in your home life that you'll be feeling most undermined, unappreciated and uneasy, and for a while it seems as though there's nothing certain in your life any more. Don't take your doubts and worries too seriously, for you're gazing on the black side and forgetting all about the bright side.

FRIDAY, 3rd. Wan, weary and plain worn out, that's you this Friday, and if you don't get a decent break soon you'll never fully recharge your batteries. There may be pressing domestic chores and odd jobs awaiting your industrious attention, but for once let duty take a back seat and simply put your feet up, for you'll be good for nothing if you don't look after yourself properly.

SATURDAY, 4th. I hope you've been cultivating your relationships and opening up your world to new partnerships, for there's lots of luck heading your way via the enthusiastic aid of folk you've taken under your wing. If you're a solitary Goat all is not lost, for there's such a sociable set of stars shining on you now that you can easily form new and very fortunate links and friendships with almost anyone you encounter. Mix and mingle – it all gives Dame Fortune a helping hand.

SUNDAY, 5th. You've had such a lot on your mind lately you could really do without the wheedling and whining ways of a fretful youngster. You may have to speak pretty sharply to them before bedtime, but don't let a quarrel carry on too long. A creative idea concerning a pet project of yours may seem absolutely brilliant at first glance, but think it over carefully before you go ahead, as you may not have seen all the angles.

MONDAY, 6th. Grab your partner by the hand and prepare to waltz your way through the dance of life in glorious good humour today! Married Goats could find their other half bursts forth with a zest for living and loving that will warm the cockles of your heart. If you're a loner by nature you'll find plenty of beaux or belles to join in with any high jinks!

TUESDAY, 7th. A fanatical friend stirs some intense emotions into activity under Tuesday's fervent sky and you'll be primed to launch yourself into an obsessive support of the cause you've espoused. It's all very well being committed to an idea shared with folk you respect, but you must keep control of your feelings, as they're inclined to get a mite overpowering and could lead you out on a limb which will be very difficult to climb down from later.

WEDNESDAY, 8th. Worries and burdens have been weighing on your mind and if you don't learn to relax and give yourself a break you'll be undermining your health and testing your nerves to the limit. Tend your body with a little pampering this Wednesday and if you have an ailment or two don't delay – consult a professional who can soon put you right.

THURSDAY, 9th. Nostalgia may not be all it used to be, but that won't stop you from indulging in a few mellow memories Thursday. It could be a certain melody heard on the radio or a particular scent wafted in on the breeze, and bingo, you're off in a delicious daydream that has nothing to do with the here and now. So long as you don't make the mistake of thinking that this mundane weekday is the be-all and end-all, this can be a wonderfully wistful and dreamy day.

FRIDAY, 10th. You're not one for trivial chitchat, and just now you have even less patience than usual with the super-ficialities of life, for you want to get right down to the heart of the matter and will appreciate anyone prepared for some straight talking. Don't expect to solve any problems in a personal project overnight, but you can iron out some worrying wrinkles today.

SATURDAY, 11th. These days your love life is beginning to look like a melodramatic romantic novel as you and your other half face storm and tempest hand in hand. Some of the wilder winds blowing through your personal life now may threaten to force you apart unless you can both come to terms with the fact that you must be free to live your own lives as well as continuing as a couple. Don't make any lasting decision solely on the basis of today's impetuous impulses, but you must be ready to jump at any chances coming your way now.

SUNDAY, 12th. What are your true standards and ideals in this life? Deep down you know that there are personal principles concerning the way this world is organised that are very important to you, and you can no longer stand by and do nothing. Don't take the whole burden of a social conscience on to your own shoulders, though, for your other half is equally concerned about current issues and will be happy to join you in your campaign.

MONDAY, 13th. As irritable Martian rays rattle the easy-going equanimity of Mother Moon on Monday you can expect a time of edgy, uptight and anxious contact with the people you meet. A child will prove particularly cantankerous and cranky but before you mete out an on-the-spot punishment check to see that they're not simply overtired. Steer clear of controversy on this argumentative day.

TUESDAY, 14th. If you're dealing with finances, tax affairs or perhaps the accounts of a group you belong to, you'll be intrigued by a scheme that seems to offer big returns for very little outlay. Now, you know very well that you don't get 'owt for nowt' in this world, but you're apt to forget this basic law. Check out a friend's advice down to the tiniest sentence of small print, for there must be a catch somewhere.

WEDNESDAY, 15th. Dealing with or sorting out other people's possessions and valuables will take up much of the next month. There's a long list of things to attend to, from joint bank balances to spending sprees and tax affairs, and you're the sensible soul who can be trusted to set everything in order. Your private life is spun from a web of intrigue which will end in a very loving and passionate period.

THURSDAY, 16th. If it strikes you that education is the key to all progress, whether in business or wisdom, you'd be quite right, and today you should look for ways to improve your own store of knowledge and information. It's a pleasure in itself to exercise your grey matter, but you could also find that constructive thought is of value in helping you to make the grade in your career and your more personal ambitions. Learning can unlock many doors!

FRIDAY, 17th. If you're one of those well-born Goats with friends in high places, exploit that advantage for all it's worth now and you'll soon be sitting pretty in a pecuniary or professional sense. You're not all such fortunate Capricorns, but I'll bet there are secret strings you can pull or contacts you can utilise to help advance an application or appeal. There's no shame in using all the resources at your disposal, whether private or public.

SATURDAY, 18th. Professionally you're at a crossroads, and few things are more likely to make a career-minded Capricorn uneasy and unsettled. There's no easy solution to the heavenly demand that you reassess your life's direction in the light of a new spiritual awareness, but if you proceed with sensitivity and caution you'll be sitting pretty when the dust finally settles. Is a sensitive soul at work helping you at the expense of their own progress?

SUNDAY, 19th. Don't be led astray by a friend who wants you to do certain things you know aren't good for you. They could exploit you sexually or even play games with your finances. Worst of all, they may take you for granted, a sin of momentous proportions to any right-minded Capricorn.

MONDAY, 20th. Supremely sensible and practical rays dart down from the heavens and decree that it's high time you got the nuts and bolts of your world in tip-top working order. You'd be wise to obey, as now you can accomplish with ease tasks that would be difficult and demanding at any other time.

TUESDAY, 21st. It's obvious (to me!) as the summer solstice shines that you should put more and more energy into your relationships. Playing mums and dads appeals to most Goats, so if you're still single go out and find yourself a luscious and lasting mate. If you're already hitched, all well and good – now's the time to replight your troth and demonstrate your gratitude to your beloved.

WEDNESDAY, 22nd. Even if the love of your life showers you with romantic reminders of their undying passion Wednesday you'll find it very difficult to get into the spirit of things, for your mind is firmly focused on some pressing practical problems. Do try to express a little affection to your other half, even though it could be a bit of an uphill struggle to disregard more down-to-earth difficulties.

THURSDAY, 23rd. Dance, music, beauty – indeed anything that you consider glamorous and gorgeous – are what you should be aiming your life at Thursday. Although you are a somewhat modest sign and shun the limelight it's time for you to take a bow, or at least show your appreciation for folk who put on a show for you. Spend time cultivating your artistic potential today.

FRIDAY, 24th. If there's one thing that canny Capricorns can be relied on for, it's sound and practical common sense. It may sound old-fashioned, but then again you're such an old-fashioned soul at heart! Today you can sweep the board, dazzle all opposition and banish all confusion simply by cutting right to the heart of any problems and clearing away the cobwebs with a few well-chosen words. If your other half has been fretting about the troubles in a friend's life, it might be worth pointing out that it is their life to do with as they wish, and carefully cutting through the tangles that confuse those close to you.

SATURDAY, 25th. The weekend's here and there's no mistaking the wonderful aura of fun that envelops you and your kin. You'll feel as though a great weight has lifted from your shoulders now and you can relax and enjoy this respite with gladness in your heart. If social frolics are your cup of tea then prepare to race to your favourite nightspot for some truly memorable revelry!

SUNDAY, 26th. What a splendid Sunday! Your superlative stars radiate good fortune and so much social success that your fame may well spread far beyond your usual boundaries. Watch out for a tall dark stranger bearing gifts from afar . . . That sounds silly, but it's via contacts with a wide range of folk from every kind of background that you'll discover your own little piece of auspicious action. It could mean amour, an opportunity to travel or a pal with professional clout. Teamwork is the key in all spheres of your life!

MONDAY, 27th. In your heart of hearts it's stability and tradition that claim your loyalty, but even you can't ignore the need to strike out and step beyond the rules once in a while. That's just what you should be doing now, as you have an urgent need to express yourself as a unique individual rather than as a cog in the social machine. Follow the path of freedom at once, as it can do you nothing but good.

TUESDAY, 28th. You seem to be caught up in an unsavoury affair this tangled Tuesday, so the sooner you can get yourself out of an undermining or ultimately destructive situation before it really takes root the better. This is a catalytic time so, by fair means or foul, if you know a person or situation isn't for you, get away before you get hurt.

WEDNESDAY, 29th. You'll find heaps of happiness in your home Wednesday, for there's an atmosphere that'll make you as snug as a bug in a rug! Anything from a romantic candlelit dinner to a more raucous rave-up will ensure fantastic fun and frolics, for this is a fine time to

celebrate or just announce your fervent feelings for someone very close. Give in to an impulse to beautify your
abode, as your taste is terrific today!

THURSDAY, 30th. Quite frankly you've had your fill of
trouble and strife so far this week, and all you crave now is a
quiet life of peaceful pleasure. I don't see why you
shouldn't put pending problems to one side just for a day so
you can recharge your physical and emotional batteries.
Maybe your other half will whisk you off for an evening's
entertainment that'll cheer you up no end? Or perhaps a
quiet night in is more your line? Take it easy, Capricorn!

JULY

FRIDAY, 1st. I know you're no stranger to steamy interludes, but perhaps you are beginning to get carried away by
it all? You love to be loved, and see no reason why you
shouldn't indulge your particular penchant for pleasure to
the full – and, after all, who could blame you for taking
advantage of such a fabulously favourable time of fulsome
fun?

SATURDAY, 2nd. Mini Mercury makes his businesslike
way into your solar house of work and wellbeing Saturday,
ushering in a potent period for professional discussions of
all kinds. If you're at all dissatisfied with your treatment,
conditions or pay at work, now's the time to put your
complaints in writing. Capricorns in search of employment
should write letters, make phone calls and attend appointments. Investigate any ailment and aim for total fitness.

SUNDAY, 3rd. The energetic entrance of mighty Mars into
your solar house of health and work from Sunday shakes

your complacency with your current occupation, for you know full well you're capable of a much more challenging role. Whether you're looking for your first toehold on the ladder to success or hoping to break through into the big time, you've the drive and determination at your fingertips now to set the ball rolling. Don't be so keen on making your mark and beating the competition that you ignore the pleasant small things that make life worth living, though.

MONDAY, 4th. Magical Moonlight is enchantingly enhanced by the voluptuous vibes of velvet Venus this Monday, turning all passionate Capricorns' minds to thoughts of amour! If you can linger in a loving embrace with the object of your desires you'll make the most of today's tender rays. On a less personal front, you have the divine diplomacy required to resolve a dispute between colleagues, customers or clients with the minimum fuss and maximum goodwill.

TUESDAY, 5th. Propose a practical solution to your partner and he or she will leap at the chance to set your shared world in apple-pie order. Any muddles or misunderstandings between you can be brought out into the cold light of day now and dealt with so quickly and easily that you'll wonder what all the fuss was about. Keep your mind on the nuts and bolts of life now.

WEDNESDAY, 6th. Mini Mercury's detour comes to an end Wednesday, helping you to begin unravelling some of the knots and tangles that have been building up amongst your friends, colleagues and employers. It's a good day to rid yourself of any doubts or grudges that may have been bothering you.

THURSDAY, 7th. You can get to the heart of the most intimate matters today without any embarrassment or humiliation. Discretion and polite enquiries will help you to get answers without any unseemly kerfuffle erupting as a result. Everything from your sex life to your dealings with the Inland Revenue can be dealt with directly under Thursday's sensitive and searching stars.

FRIDAY, 8th. A wonderful watershed is reached in your one-to-one affairs today. Weddings, anniversaries and any-thing that galvanises two people into a team are a must. Those involved in business partnerships are also given an astral incentive to make pacts or sign agreements, for Fri-day's luscious lunar rays underline the basic goodness of all relationships for security-conscious Goats.

SATURDAY, 9th. The witty repartee will be flying through the air with startling speed Saturday as you and your other half are simultaneously hit by a restless mood that sets your tongues wagging nineteen to the dozen. The trouble is that neither of you wants to stop talking long enough to listen, and that's when the frustration begins to build up a head of steam. For goodness' sake, act like mature adults and at least take it in turns to natter on about your exciting ideas!

SUNDAY, 10th. Mercury the messenger slips back into your solar house of one-to-one affairs from Sunday and promptly sets your and your partner's tongues wagging again. Until 3 August you've a splendid opportunity to oil the wheels of your relationships with a few well-placed words and astute observations. It may be your spouse, a boss or your best friend who need reassuring – all it takes is a few kind words and a willingness to listen as well as talk. Communication is the crucial key to harmony in all your partnerships, romantic or not!

MONDAY, 11th. The gentle stars are softly twinkling with a tender light, making this a time to draw close to the one you love. A reunion or nostalgic trip embarked on now will bring back many sweet and happy memories. You may decide to return to a place that will evoke your thoughts and feelings in a most sentimental way, warming the cockles of your heart through and through.

TUESDAY, 12th. A lovely time is predicted for you now if you cash in on the trends around you. Your love life has a crystal-clear ring to it, whilst travel on any level will bring you a well-deserved respite. A time to go out into the world. Best foot forward, Capricorn!

WEDNESDAY, 13th. Open your eyes this morning and thank your lucky stars that all the storm clouds have cleared away for the moment, leaving you with the confident conviction that your problems can be easily solved and swiftly banished! It may be a new warmth and affection in your relationship with your other half, or an understanding you've reached with an adversary that's given you this optimistic outlook. Whatever it is, it'll help you to look on the bright side.

THURSDAY, 14th. Everything seemed so clear yesterday, but today the storm clouds have closed in around you and the love of your life once more. You try to get through, but it's just as though you're talking in different languages for all the good it's doing. Don't jump to any catastrophic conclusions about the state of your close personal relationships under such a misty and murky sky, for the chances are you've grabbed the wrong end of the stick.

FRIDAY, 15th. Have you been giving your other half their fair quota of attention and affection? If not you'll soon know about it today as they pout their way through breakfast or turn a deaf ear to your casual comments. Take the hint and treat them to a lavish evening spent entirely in your charming company. It'll thrill them to bits! Solo Goats should make sure the pressure of work isn't keeping you from a full social life.

SATURDAY, 16th. Your future hopes and wishes take a definite turn for the better today. Help from a woman or advice from an important man will be all you need to get that little twinkle back in your eye, and the celestial signal is that nothing is as bad as it seems.

SUNDAY, 17th. Where your relationships are concerned this hasn't been the most peaceful period, and Sunday sees another storm blowing up out of nowhere as you and your other half start to lash out wildly in a bid for freedom. Things have been getting a wee bit stale and dull, and you both need a breath of fresh air, so rather than have a row about it why not take off into the wide blue yonder and do something completely different together? Variety really is the spice of life!

MONDAY, 18th. It's a superb period for you to look at your future and at last realise where you're going. You may have to make certain changes to any formulas or plans you have, but that's only to be expected, for this is a time when the world as you know it is being transfigured in some way. The power of Pluto will help you to transform monstrosities into marvellous creations.

TUESDAY, 19th. Sound common sense is the hallmark of Tuesday as far as canny Capricorns are concerned. Clouds of confusion flee before your penetrating insight now. To you, of course, the solutions to quandries are just obvious, but don't underestimate the knack. Those in your close circle will be astounded by the speed with which you unravel the knots of any issue.

146

WEDNESDAY, 20th. You're keen to travel, and endlessly inquisitive about the way other people live in different parts of the world, but if you're actually journeying today you shouldn't expect everything to run like clockwork or to schedule. Delays due to circumstances beyond your control are more than likely, so don't be too impatient to get from A to B. Remember, it's better to travel hopefully than to arrive!

THURSDAY, 21st. The more you try to have a head-on discussion with a loved one about the practicalities of life the more you're likely to be beating your head against a brick wall. You're not known as the most subtle sign of the zodiac for nothing, though, so with a little delicate negotiation you'll be able to tackle a subject that sorely needs attention.

FRIDAY, 22nd. The lunar clock strikes full in your Sun sign today as the time has arrived for important personal decisions and diversions. It's now that you must apply the full stop to a chapter in your novel of life as you're about to turn over a new leaf. To do this, however, there are many out-of-date situations that must be discarded without regret or reluctance.

SATURDAY, 23rd. It may be high summer, but for you the Sun's sensational light is dimmed and muted for a wee while as he sinks into the area of your horoscope relating to secretive, sensitive and sexual affairs. Far from prying eyes, you're preparing for a sizzling series of erotic encounters and intimate interludes. There's a glint of gold in the heavens too, helping you to forge ahead in any delicate negotiations designed to enrich you and yours.

SUNDAY, 24th. Mentally you're an inspired and uplifted wee Goat as you begin to see a way to achieve a new way of thinking and expressing yourself that's more in tune with the times. Talk over ways of combining the ideals of compassion and charity with a sensible and practical approach to the world and you'll be in for a splendid sense of satisfaction.

MONDAY, 25th. A grey cloud covers the heavens and puts the brakes on travel and communications in your world today. You'll need to exercise patience as messages go astray and phone calls are misunderstood and interrupted. It's a very fleeting phase, and you'll soon be back on form, so don't take it all too seriously.

TUESDAY, 26th. You're in danger of losing your cold and crusty image altogether this Tuesday as nebulous Neptunian vibes continue to emphasise your soft-hearted and sensitive side. Instead of concentrating on the superficial meaning of today's meetings and messages, let your imagination roam into the realm of conjecture where you'll pick up on hidden clues to folk's motivations. Are you sure you're not psychic?

WEDNESDAY, 27th. Tact and plain good taste come to your rescue and enable you to smooth down the most ruffled and windswept feathers in no time at all. An in-depth discussion ranging over many topics with your loved one will reveal many points of agreement and strengthen your bond thereby. If you're treading a solitary line you should mix and mingle now as amour could be about to enter the scene.

THURSDAY, 28th. Anyone would think that you'd be all talked out by now, but you haven't run out of words and ideas yet. It could be that it's the other folk in your world who are beginning to feel the mental pace of the last few days, so don't be too offended if they tell you to put a sock in it for a while. You probably need to pause for breath anyway, and while you're at it you can take some time to digest the cornucopia of new ideas at your beck and call.

FRIDAY, 29th. It has been claimed that Capricorns keep a tight grip on the purse strings. 'Never a borrower or a lender be' is a phrase that you've whipped straight out of *Hamlet* and given a home in your heart. Today, though, that proverbial canniness with the cash deserts you as you dig deep in your pocket to help out a friend. But before your better nature is stirred, ask yourself if this supposed need is actually genuine, or is a liberty being taken? Make enquiries before parting with any of your hard-earned resources.

SATURDAY, 30th. Today is one of those highly mystical, magical and mysterious days when only the most enlightened and sensitive of you will feel the full range of the vague vibrations surrounding you. If you want to understand more about your inner world of the unconscious and the imagination, this is a fine time to delve deep. But don't make the mistake of thinking folk will understand your otherworldly insights! Someone who feigns a close interest in your spiritual development may be bluffing.

SUNDAY, 31st. 'Marry in haste, repent at leisure' goes the old saying, and Sunday that applies to even the most stick-in-the-mud Capricorn, as you're liable to let your tongue run away with you and could end up blurting out all sorts of wild statements and promises to your other half that you'll regret tomorrow. Make sure that you have plenty of new ideas and experiences to assimilate, and you won't be quite as restless and reckless in your speech.

AUGUST

MONDAY, 1st. Your imagination is very vivid now, which is great if you're a Goat who likes to while away the hours painting, sewing, knitting or the like, but if you're feeling unsettled or troubled there's a likelihood that self-deception or escapism could have an adverse effect. Your partnership needs to face up to the truth, and you could be the one to show him or her the way to a more honest openness.

TUESDAY, 2nd. The keynote of this whole period is one of expanded horizons and tastes in your convictions and beliefs about all that's of value and beauty in this world. An unexpected encounter, perhaps with an exotic soul from foreign parts, will take your education in life a stage further and open your eyes to many new ways of living that you've rejected before. I know it's an effort, but you must keep an open and tolerant mind to reap the benefits.

WEDNESDAY, 3rd. You'd better get any important letters in the post now, for Mercury's progress through the zodiac introduces an aura of magic and mystery that'll cause confusion in all communications. A discreet approach from someone in business could give you plenty of productive financial ideas, so be prepared to follow up the most subtle and secretive of clues in the coming weeks.

THURSDAY, 4th. A friend who appears to have rather more than a purely platonic interest in you is mightily impressed with your upright and ethical stance on a moral issue and may volunteer their services to help you promote and publicise your principles. Even if a romance is out of the question you'll be deeply moved by their devotion, for together you stand an excellent chance of achieving your most exalted objectives.

FRIDAY, 5th. Your attention may be captured by an item of news that seems to you symptomatic of the society we live in today. Maybe it's time you took a hand in shaping tomorrow's world? However small your contribution, from giving to charity to joining a pressure group, it'll do you good to know you're active and involved.

SATURDAY, 6th. As you flick through the glossy adverts aimed at encouraging investments, savings or pension plans, it all looks too good to be true. Maybe that's because people are indeed bending the truth just a tiny bit to tempt you out on to a financial limb! You'll be left hanging on to an overloaded budgetary branch for dear life if you believe all you hear or read today.

SUNDAY, 7th. Whatever you class as your career begins a beneficial period when harmony reigns and you can bridge any gaps between you and your employer. You could do worse than to wine and dine someone who can help you attain your ambitions, or pull some strings that will put you on the right professional tracks. A powerful woman is on your side and you have the winning ways to keep her there!

MONDAY, 8th. On a purely mental level you know there are some very positive reasons to hope for a better world in the future, but your heart is at variance with your head as you react emotionally to some gloomy news Monday. It may be an overdramatised story in the media or a more personal problem that's bringing you down, but before you assume the worst, wait for confirmation. Things will look much brighter when you have all the relevant information.

TUESDAY, 9th. Current affairs capture your attention this Tuesday. Maybe you've a personal interest in the way an international situation is developing, or have come to realise how crucial a broader understanding of the world is to developing a more convincing creed? Listening to TV documentaries, radio reports and reading last Sunday's papers from cover to cover will all help to put you in the picture. Be a well-informed Capricorn!

WEDNESDAY, 10th. Unemployed Goats will find that a vocation that is artistic, for the good of women or connected with entertainment should be pursued now. Any of these will suit those of you who are simply fed up with your career, too.

THURSDAY, 11th. Though I'm not one to encourage listening at keyholes, or dropping any eaves, a remark overheard in the workplace will put you in an advantageous position. If you've been trying to persuade an employer or autocratic authority figure of your worth, then a little leverage might just come in handy. Remember that a secret shared isn't a secret any more, so keep tight-lipped and act on what you learn now!

FRIDAY, 12th. A clandestine conference or perhaps just a subtle hint from someone in a position of power and authority can give you good reason to set your sights on the very top of your professional tree. If you're an unemployed and dissatisfied Goat you should be prepared to talk to all and sundry about your talents and skills, as news will trickle through and enhance your prospects.

SATURDAY, 13th. You're astrally endowed with all the *joie de vivre* and social savvy required to cut a delightful dash amongst your buddies this Saturday. With a little initiative and enterprise you should be able to get a wee gathering organised so you can enjoy the enthusiastic adulation of your adoring fans! A fantastic day for cheering up an old chum and forming new friendships.

SUNDAY, 14th. A firm friend shows an interest in your private life and sets up a reaction that will have you withdrawing from all contact due simply to embarrassment and a desire to keep certain things confidential. You may be right to shield your privacy but are you sure you're not overreacting? Give them another chance, as it would be a shame to lose a friend over such a trivial incident.

MONDAY, 15th. Even a usually taciturn Goat like you has days when your tongue seems to have a will of its own and secrets spill from your lips with alarming regularity. When the realities of life, such as money, are discussed, it's very easy to disclose too many personal facts now, so try to keep tight-lipped when the subject of 'the root of all evil' crops up. Confidences are made to be kept and you'll only have yourself to blame if a friend's circumstances are revealed in embarrassing detail!

TUESDAY, 16th. There's always a danger when Mars, the planet of the self, marches into the house in your solar horoscope devoted to relationships. The obvious problem is that one or t'other of you is interested only in 'I', whilst the other is striving towards 'We'! This could lead to a spring of discontent unless compromise flushes out selfishness, so seek a diplomatic solution.

WEDNESDAY, 17th. Mother Moon's being driven to distraction by the needling rays of martial Mars, making you on edge, irritable and liable to snap at your spouse or anyone who makes a false move. It hardly seems fair when you're trying to be reasonable, for it seems some folk are out to get you riled this Wednesday. Foil their fiendish plot by keeping cool, calm and collected – it'll drive them wild instead!

THURSDAY, 18th. Your mind is opened to new thoughts and very adventurous ideas, but be warned of religious extremists or political activists who misguidedly try to convert you. Anything taken too much to heart can get out of control and cause you to question everything from the most trivial to the most traditional. A challenging period demanding mental growth and expansion.

FRIDAY, 19th. There's something funny going on in the background, especially if you're engaged in large-scale legal or financial dealings. Everything looks perfectly proper on the surface, but you didn't get where you are today by being taken in by slick operators, so don't hesitate to check figures, follow up contacts and cross-reference credentials. You could uncover a racket that's been undermining your pecuniary position for some time.

SATURDAY, 20th. You need a wee pause to catch your breath after the buffeting you received yesterday, so try not to fill your appointments book with too many urgent meetings. You're not up to tackling much in the way of business and would be wise to just let things tick over for a while to allow you to stand back and think things through. Understanding folk at work will back you up.

SUNDAY, 21st. Money must take the spotlight in your life now, from sorting out what you've got to finding out how you can make more. But if things get too material, a wise Goat remembers that our values must also be counted in spiritual ways. If you're unhappy and fretful, perhaps it's because you're not placing enough emphasis on your spiritual worth and resources.

MONDAY, 22nd. There's a starry pattern interwoven around your solar house of philosophy and higher-mindedness that will help you expand and grow intellectually quite beautifully. A fortuitous time for all education, study or activities with a cultural flavour.

TUESDAY, 23rd. You'll be tempted to throw caution to the wind as Tuesday's scintillating celestial sensation fills you with a burning desire to expand your personal horizons and venture into uncharted territories. Plan an off-the-cuff journey or take up some comprehensive and challenging reading matter. Shake free of the boring old limits of the everyday world for a while – it'll be an invigorating experience.

WEDNESDAY, 24th. You're still locked in a dispute with your kith and kin, as you all insist in having your own way and no one seems willing to give an inch. The conflict will spread to your close personal relationships if you're not careful, so maybe you should call in an independent referee to keep the peace and sort out the tangled web of claim and counter-claim. A tiresome day, but with some self-control peace is attainable.

THURSDAY, 25th. However hard you try to put a brave face on the need to meet your obligations Thursday, you'd really much prefer to let duties fall. In fact it won't hurt your professional image at all to let your home-loving leanings show, so don't struggle too much to keep mega-cool. Anyone who thought you were hard-boiled will see your super-soft centre today!

FRIDAY, 26th. All revved up and raring to go! That's your mood this Friday when you feel ready to tackle a mountain of paperwork or run around on some urgent errands – all before breakfast! Make the most of your brilliant turn of speed and pack in plenty of the tasks you normally find tiresome and tedious. You'll get them done in record time! Don't be so busy with the day's business you forget to have fun.

SATURDAY, 27th. Go into Saturday with a practical, suspicious and sceptical air and you'll be fine, but drop your defences for one moment and there'll be folk spinning yarns as long as the Lancashire cotton looms and tales taller than the Empire State Building. If you take anyone at face value you'll end up demoralised and disillusioned, so it's a case of steady as she goes!

SUNDAY, 28th. Your justly famed practical nature can make the most of all opportunities today. A casual hint dropped by a colleague or relative will find some fertile ground in your imagination, firing your enthusiasm and setting your active mind on course to a marvellous achievement. A long-held wish will come a step nearer to fulfilment because now you'll know exactly what you have to do to make your dreams a reality!

MONDAY, 29th. Common sense is all very well in its place but there are times when you need to stretch intellectually beyond the rigid boundaries of what's possible in order to speculate and wonder. Enquire into your own spiritual convictions and religious beliefs now, for you need to know where you stand on certain philosophical or ethical issues. If all you encounter is a lot of questions and no answers, seek out someone who's thought things through more thoroughly.

TUESDAY, 30th. Goats on vacation should take a detour from the beaten track, whether you're in some exotic location or enjoying the sensational scenery of this sceptred isle, for by being a wee bit more adventurous you could add so much more to the benefits to be gained from your holiday. If you're stuck at home, indulge in a little intellectual exploration by finding out more about an unusual subject that interests you, such as astrology!

WEDNESDAY, 31st. The cosmic energies around you today are second to none. Your relationships look good enough to eat, and the only way anything will go wrong will be if you put on a superior attitude. You can take a chance and gamble with a person's feelings and *still* come out smiling.

SEPTEMBER

THURSDAY, 1st. Current affairs capture your attention once more as a pal who knows your interests brings you a snippet of information about plans in the offing. It could be local developments or a nationwide campaign you're keen to join, but whatever gets your goat you're not willing to stand by and do nothing. Relieve your fevered feelings by dashing off a pointed missive to your MP or contacting your local rag for a little extra publicity.

FRIDAY, 2nd. Colour and vitality drain from your world as you begin to feel that you're up against insuperable odds. You need to find a way of expressing your more compassionate impulses, but wherever you turn you meet with a demoralising muddle that will soon convince you that nobody understands and that you're all alone. Not a day to attempt too much.

SATURDAY, 3rd. There's more than a touch of jollity today for all Capricorns as the splendid light of the sun mingles harmoniously with the genial rays of giant Jupiter. A reunion with an old friend and a chance to catch up on old news and create some new memories is likely. A happy weekend atmosphere prevails at a time when fun and a less-than-serious mood will take the edge off your crusty Capricorn reputation. This is a good time for packing your bags for an impromptu trip, because a change of scene will do you the world of good!

SUNDAY, 4th. An intelligent appraisal of your career and ambition prospects is called for, and now that mini Mercury brings his marvellous mental rays back to your house of professional aspirations you have the wit and wisdom to proceed with your analysis. Appointments, meetings and messages related to your position in the world will start to flood in, setting off a busy and bustling period when you can make many valuable contacts.

MONDAY, 5th. The New Moon today places a profound planetary pressure on you to reassess your most basic beliefs. Brand-new doctrines being promoted now run counter to your previous principles, but that's no reason to dismiss them out of hand. Maybe it's time you brought your personal creed up to date? After all, this is the 1990s and modern scientific knowledge has to be taken into account. You're on the verge of a spiritual sea change or religious reformation!

TUESDAY, 6th. A lovely lunar light illuminates your world and diverts your attention from any everyday concerns. It's questions of faith and more profound beliefs that attract you now, as your feelings reflect a greater spiritual awareness. You needn't worry about neglecting practical affairs, for it's your inner state of mind that takes planetary priority.

WEDNESDAY, 7th. The luscious lady of the skies, velvet Venus, steps into your solar house of future hopes and coaxes you into admitting that you do have a romantic ideal or two tucked away beneath that craggy exterior! If you can't seem to achieve perfection just yet, don't be disheartened, as your social life is imbued with a rosy glow of romance that promises plenty of pleasure in the weeks ahead.

THURSDAY, 8th. Calmness and clarity certainly shouldn't be expected Thursday, as nebulous Neptune casts a magic spell and throws your emotions into an even greater confusion. You're hypersensitive to the slightest criticism or comment from folk in authority and as a result you'll begin to doubt anything and everything. Take it easy and don't tackle too much just now.

FRIDAY, 9th. As soon as the working day ends you'll be gearing yourself to party! Yes, the weekend is here and you'll be ready, willing and able to make the most of it. When the magical Moon teams up with jovial Jupiter it's time to set your feet tapping to the rhythm of frivolity. Forget petty worries and head for the bright lights to spend some quality time with friends old and new.

SATURDAY, 10th. Normally your actions are determined by purely practical, common-sense considerations, but just this once you should take heed of a hunch you have over the correct course in a question about your career. Any officials you deal with now will be so touched by your apparent care and compassion that they'll be ready to go out of their way to help you attain your targets.

SUNDAY, 11th. After an action-packed weekend you'd think that what's needed is a day's relative rest, but you're raring to go once more, packed to the go-ahead gills with vim, vigour and vitality! It could be the encouragement of your other half making all the difference, or a friend with a rousing line in pep talks who's got you ducking and diving, ready to take on the entire world. Whatever, it's a sensational Sunday for setting your social circle in a spin with your entertaining initiatives.

MONDAY, 12th. If the wicked ways of the world are beginning to discourage, dishearten and depress you, why not forget just for once about your efforts to show people the error of their ways? You're in such an ultra-sensitive state just now and need to protect yourself from the rough and tumble of debate, so turn down any intriguing offers to defend your principles. You'll persuade far more effectively through setting an example anyhow!

TUESDAY, 13th. Your social life is certainly sizzling these days! Party-going Goats are in for a terrific time meeting fresh friends, talking over old times with long-term buddies and generally dancing the light fantastic! If your appointment diary's bare, invite some pals to your place for a wee get-together or nip into your local pub, club or nightspot. You need to feel part of a merry crowd, and with your sparkling personality that's easy!

WEDNESDAY, 14th. You're not really *au fait* with what's going on around you and are getting lulled into a false sense of security, but it's nothing to get uptight about. Try to realise that you're going through one of the most spiritual phases of your life. It won't just stop here, for the trends are long and drawn out, changing lifelong patterns of beliefs and faith.

THURSDAY, 15th. There seems to be an inbuilt principle of chaos involved with money, as however many times you think you've closed every loophole and set up a foolproof system something comes along to upset the apple-cart. Your bank balance is way out of line, and you don't know what's gone wrong, so you're off on the trail of monetary errors yet again. Persevere and you'll soon make things watertight again.

FRIDAY, 16th. Culturally your natural inclination is to value the tried and tested traditional styles that are generally respected and acknowledged as the best, but a perverse fancy is taking you lately and you realise that more rebellious forms of art and thought can have much to offer. You're not exactly out to shock folk with your avant-garde tastes, but you don't mind causing a few raised eyebrows as you declare your interests!

SATURDAY, 17th. A word of wisdom from a serious-minded friend could calm down the most fevered brow this Saturday. If the complications of your emotional life have got you in a turmoil, then rest assured that the most complex issue can be laid to rest by some simple applications of sound common sense. As a Capricorn you know that the cool light of reason solves most things in this world, but when affairs of the heart are involved the waters can get murky. Allow someone you trust to clear the picture for you!

SUNDAY, 18th. There's no way you can possibly put anything extra into your partnerships unless you have total faith in your other half. Perhaps something is niggling you about them; you may even feel they're up to something behind your back; but whatever it is that makes you uneasy don't avoid any issues or sweep your feelings under the carpet. Be honest and open, Capricorn.

MONDAY, 19th. A travel opportunity that seems on the surface to be no more than a jolly little jaunt could turn out to have far more impact on your life than you could have suspected, but don't worry – it's all in the nicest possible way! If a journey is out of the question you should mix and mingle with folk who can put you in touch with distant shores, as it's through stretching your ideas now that you'll progress.

TUESDAY, 20th. A bright idea from someone in the know will set off a train of thought in your own mind that gathers so much momentum as it goes along that pretty soon you'll be thinking too fast for your own good! Don't try to restrict such a creative flow, but instead make notes of the more brilliant brainwaves so that you can think them through more thoroughly when you're mentally more astute and settled. Potentially this is an enormously creative day when routine should be disregarded as much as possible.

WEDNESDAY, 21st. Self-centred Mars and rebellious Uranus face up to each other across the heavens today and engage in a titanic struggle for supremacy that will be sending shock waves into all corners of the globe. It's your one-to-one partnerships that take the brunt of the almighty argument, as you too are determined to have things your own way and just won't take no for an answer. This is no way to decide a crucial issue, but things have come to a boil and the steam has to go somewhere.

THURSDAY, 22nd. If you turn some of your startlingly unusual artistic attentions on to your abode you will be tempted to change things round in a radical rearrangement that will have your kith and kin gaping open-mouthed as they wonder just what's got into you. It's just that you're sick of being a stick-in-the-mud Capricorn, always doing things by the book, and why shouldn't you have a fling every so often? Before you paint the kitchen puce or the living room bright yellow, though, perhaps you'd better reflect for a moment on whether you'll be able to actually live with the new decor!

FRIDAY, 23rd. Your professional prospects can rocket sky-high if you take your established experience and interlace it with your unique and inventive personality. Don't denigrate yourself or hold back from the full flood of ideas welling up inside you, as you're in cracking creative form. Any career or occupation can only benefit from your steadfast but go-ahead outlook, for the heavens in the month ahead are granting you a passport to fame and fortune.

SATURDAY, 24th. The storm clouds clear away just as quickly as they developed today, leaving you basking in the super Sunshine of the very harmonious heavens. It's with your frolicsome friends that you're in your entertaining element now, keeping folk rolling in the aisles with your sardonic comments and charming every new acquaintance coming within your range. Just don't hog the limelight!

SUNDAY, 25th. You may not exactly be a fitness fanatic but that's no excuse for neglecting your physique, especially if you hope to make a good impression on a potential employer or patron. Is your diet all it should be, and do you get enough exercise? Ask yourself some searching questions and adopt a more healthy regime now, for with just a little effort you can easily achieve the body beautiful.

163

MONDAY, 26th. If there are social problems and community concerns that strike you as urgent and alarming, now's the time to get together with like-minded folk to organise a campaign. You'll succeed beyond your wildest dreams. Go for it, Capricorn!

TUESDAY, 27th. Young master Mercury, the baby of the solar system, skips into your solar house related to your future wishes and from today ushers in a busy period when you'll be overflowing with bright ideas designed to make this world a better place for all and sundry in the years ahead. It's a long-term perspective you'll be taking now as you attend meetings, join groups and generally throw yourself heart and soul into the gathering of like-minded souls working for a common cause.

WEDNESDAY, 28th. Friends, neighbours, relatives – today you should spend time with someone close. There is a feeling of happiness in the air so join a club, perhaps go to a whist drive or drop in for a drink at a bar on the way home. What you mustn't do is complain that nobody loves you and then do nothing about it.

THURSDAY, 29th. Thursday cannot possibly be a bad day no matter how pessimistic you feel first thing in the morning. Those two benevolent astral bodies Venus and Jupiter bestow a multitude of bountiful blessings now, and provide an uplift to your mood and your vision of life. Good friends are a joy now, and you'll be able to bring your hopes, wishes and most cherished dreams a step closer to fruition! What a lucky Capricorn!

FRIDAY, 30th. Whatever you say this Friday it seems you've rubbed your other half up the wrong way, as you're both inclined to let your hearts rule your heads. You're impatient to get on with professional duties and earthly obligations, but you'll only add to any problems if you don't give sentimental issues equal care and attention. A trying, tiring and tedious day.

OCTOBER

SATURDAY, 1st. Self-discipline goes flying out of the window as the two ladies of the skies, Venus and the Moon, get together and declare a day of sweet and sentimental indulgence. You're filled with affection for all and sundry, and only want to surround yourself with the most pleasing and pampering experiences. Not a day for demanding work, as your mind is on much finer things!

SUNDAY, 2nd. Have you been having second thoughts lately about bringing your entire image up to date? Maybe it seemed a good idea at the time but the weight of time-tested tradition has been too much for you. Well, wave goodbye to such delays and indecisions, for you're once more set celestially on course for a more modern you. Toss out clothes that hark back to the past, and buy yourself some with-it fashions to demonstrate for all the world to see that you're a contemporary Capricorn!

MONDAY, 3rd. Do you have faraway friends or remote relatives who haven't been in contact for a while? Don't sit back and wait for them to do all the running to keep in touch. They'll be thrilled if you drop them a line or put through a long-distance call and could begin to get discouraged if you don't do your bit. Don't let a lazy and listless streak sabotage your relationships.

TUESDAY, 4th. Friday brings Mars marching into his most erotic and sensuous position in your solar horoscope. Apart from fuelling your passions with a profound propulsion you will also be driven by a desire to get to grips with psychological defects and quirks that have caused hang-ups and inferiority complexes in this most intimate and private side of your life.

WEDNESDAY, 5th. They say there's no smoke without fire, and it's very hard to know which flame to pursue Wednesday. It's difficult enough for you to understand what's happening, let alone to realise that lunar rays are prompting you to come up with a new career avenue that will give you more chance of honour, prestige and success. Your ego needs a challenge before you make a public spectacle of yourself and flip your lid out of sheer frustration. Professional renewal is needed before your enthusiasm fizzles out.

THURSDAY, 6th. You have grounds Thursday to suspect that someone who's crossed swords with you in the past may be bearing a grudge and working against you from behind the scenes. A friend who alerts you to the fact may have their own reasons for stirring up trouble, so don't assume the worst until you've investigated the facts for yourself. A day of tiresome tensions.

FRIDAY, 7th. If you've been wondering how to implement some ideas aimed at improving your local environment, talk to a contact with experience of parochial politics and parish pressure groups, for they'll have some extremely sensible suggestions that'll help you devise a down-to-earth plan of action. Once you show that you're in earnest, you'll receive the backing of influential people throughout the neighbourhood.

SATURDAY, 8th. Even when you're apparently sitting back and enjoying a totally soporific and indolent Saturday, your busy mind is beavering away in the background, working out ways and means to impose your will on others! Subtle strategies are your stock in trade now, so why not put your devious skills to use for a worthy cause? Anything from raising funds for a charity to giving a few timely tips to a pal with love problems is right up your street today.

SUNDAY, 9th. Take extra care if you're transmitting important messages now, for madcap Mercury wavers and wanders off the beaten track, introducing a note of chaos and carelessness to the most uncomplicated of errands. Fortunately your friends are inclined to be patient, which is just as well, for they're equally apt to miss the point and forget important details!

MONDAY, 10th. It's possible, nay probable, that today you will formulate an idea or plan that could be taken up by someone who really believes in what you're doing. It's time to blow your own trumpet, whether by letter or verbally. A pal will also make a useful introduction to help your future.

TUESDAY, 11th. Who said that Capricorns were boring? Not me, and you've proved it, for you're a star of the social scene now! Splendid soirees and unparalleled parties are on offer to you. You'll have a fantastic time conversing with old friends and new. Your feet will be tapping as you take to the floor, proving yourself to be a regular gigolo or gigolette! If invites don't come flooding to you, don't just sit there – issue some yourself. It's time to show that Goats are real party animals!

WEDNESDAY, 12th. Unpredictable Uranian rays in your own house of personal issues will be forcing you to tune in to this modern world and there's no point in trying to insist that you're just a simple traditional soul at heart because it simply won't wash any more. The only thing outdated about you is your attitude, and that's in the process of being well and truly modernised now. You'll soon be an up-to-the-minute groovy wee Goat!

THURSDAY, 13th. There are times when it's wise to take another look at your vision of the future. Though some long-cherished desires have to change as Venus enters a wayward mood, you'll find that certain fair-weather friends aren't very sympathetic to your change of heart. Perhaps an ambition you once held doesn't have the same attraction for you any longer? From now until 23 November you have the opportunity to reassess your position and your revised aims.

FRIDAY, 14th. You Capricorns, being ambitious souls, love a task that you can get your teeth into. At the same time, you can feel your confidence draining away as you contemplate the challenge, for you're in a dreamy and delicate state and just not up to anything too demanding. Try not to schedule any important meetings or tasks as your energy is below par and you need to take it easy. Watch out for an official who's out to deceive.

SATURDAY, 15th. There's a critical and cynical atmosphere around Capricorns Saturday. You could make the lives of your nearest and dearest a total misery if you don't control your tendency to carp and criticise over any little thing. Sparks will fly as your capacity for tact is minute now. Try to examine the motives behind this irritable you. Are you sure that you aren't taking a work frustration home?

SUNDAY, 16th. Your famous patient persistence will desert you for a day as you suddenly feel like stamping your foot in frustration at the people in power who seem determined to bar your way to the higher echelons of your career or social circle. You're quite right to kick up a bit of a fuss, as it's not fair that you should always be overlooked when preferment and promotion are in the offing, but if you get too insolent and offensive you could set your cause back rather than advance it.

MONDAY, 17th. A clandestine economic issue requires urgent attention and you're the one with the know-how to deal with it effectively. It could be family finances, a tax tangle, or perhaps an inheritance that needs to be set in order, and to anyone but a careful and methodical Capricorn that could be a daunting task. Folk know that they can count on you, though, and they won't be disappointed.

TUESDAY, 18th. The nights are drawing in and you'll be thinking of the comforts of hearth and home as you start to hanker after a little home cooking and those lovely cosy evenings gathered around the fireside with your kith and kin. You're inundated with childhood memories and these evocative images bring back the times when you were happiest with your family. Bliss!

WEDNESDAY, 19th. It's time to turn your attentions to the attainment of your own ambitions, leaving more general objectives aside for the time being. Are you abreast of all the latest information in your field? Are there bosses and bigwigs you really need to bring within your area of influence? Ask yourself these and other pertinent professional questions and set about investigating your options.

A productive period for making new career contacts and tootling your own trumpet!

THURSDAY, 20th. Someone who's normally a much-loved playmate may say something out of turn this Thursday and as a result arouse your anger. With anyone else the whole problem could be over in a matter of moments, but you find it so difficult to forgive and forget. Are you going to let an offhand remark poison your entire relationship? You know it makes much better sense to simply explain your irritation and let it pass.

FRIDAY, 21st. The Sun and Mercury combine their potent forces to help you make a mark in your professional world, so make the most of this last chance to utilise the full force of their astral assistance. Just for once it won't hurt at all to talk big and put on a perfectly poised and positive perform- ance, even if it means glossing over a few awkward and embarrassing facts. With your self-assured manner you'll be taken at face value.

SATURDAY, 22nd. Yet again, you face the weekend with a mournful and melancholy look and a complete reluctance to make the required effort. Wrapping up warm to avoid the chills will help, and you could bribe yourself with the promise of an evening spent toasting your tootsies by the fire. This is one of those days when you just can't seem to get yourself motivated.

SUNDAY, 23rd. The all-powerful Sun proceeds into your solar house of hopes and wishes Sunday and whilst you're mentally charged up with such superb creative energy you should think through your objectives in life, as it's as clear as crystal to you that once personal targets have been met we all have a responsibility to do our best for society as a whole. Transforming our social system is a tall order, but every little helps and you're in a determined mood.

MONDAY, 24th. A few discreet words with your colleagues or companions will reveal a strategy for improvement in your working environment that promises a massive turn for the better. Provide those in authority, whether it's at work or in dealings with the government or local council, with evidence of your group solidarity and you'll make progress. Personal and shared ambitions are highlighted now.

TUESDAY, 25th. Committed Capricorns can look forward to a delicious day with their spouse or sweetheart. You feel completely in tune with each other, able to understand your inner needs and desires and delighting in each other's company. Friends are also important, so remember your mates. Think about future plans – you could turn a valuable vision into a pet project now.

WEDNESDAY, 26th. You're normally such a dutiful and obliging soul that folk will be more than a little stunned to see your behaviour now you've decided you've had more than your fair share of being ordered around. Anyone who tries to lord it over you will be in for an earful that isn't really fit to hear, as you're in no mood to be pushed around and won't stand for it any more. A new age of independence dawns!

THURSDAY, 27th. It's not like you to neglect or ignore monetary matters, but today you could find that an important fiscal issue has indeed been overlooked, and that could set back your plans and force you into a rethink. An investment opportunity may not be as lucrative as you were led to expect, so it's a good idea to keep a tight grip on the purse strings and possibly tighten your belt as well. You are such a canny soul usually, so you should soon be back on the right pecuniary course.

FRIDAY, 28th. Even though a recent setback has put you in a pessimistic frame of mind, the glorious rays of genial Jupiter will lift your spirits no end when they combine with the intuitive rays of dreamy Neptune. Your sensitive feelings are abundantly enhanced as you enter a much more positive and forward-looking phase. You'll get a sense that all's right with the world on this day of faith and harmony.

SATURDAY, 29th. If you've a plan in mind that requires great self-discipline and control, now's your chance as your ruler, sober Saturn, is providing a channel for the Sun's rays that will motivate you to get down to brass tacks in no uncertain terms. Organise meetings with practical pals or pick up a detailed manual or two and you'll find that by bedtime you've put a chaotic situation into order in a supremely satisfying way. You deserve a pat on the back!

SUNDAY, 30th. Red tape's been tying you in knots lately, as you've been bombarded with letters, forms and questionnaires from all kinds of official and officious sources. Go through them with a fine-tooth comb and sort out the wheat from the chaff – they may not even have anything to do with you, so don't let yourself be intimidated or get worried without good reason!

MONDAY, 31st. You may think that you've evolved the perfect plan to launch you on a career that's aimed at the very top, but you should go back and check your facts and figures right from the beginning before you make a public statement. However careful you've been you'll find that a few fatal flaws have crept in; there's a muddle at the heart of your thinking that needs to be resolved before you can proceed. It's tiresome, but you need to hold back or some Hallowe'en moonshine will tie you in knots.

NOVEMBER

TUESDAY, 1st. Secretive strategies are afoot in your professional world, and for a subtle and perceptive Goat like you there's an abundance of opportunity just waiting to be exploited. Take decisive action to further your interests now by making behind-the-scenes moves, and you'll soon be sitting very pretty!

WEDNESDAY, 2nd. You're really on the ball this Wednesday, for people you've been trying to convert suddenly make an about-turn and accept your point in principle. It could have been an appeal to their emotions as much as any rational argument you've put forward that's convinced them, so don't forget that powerful people and arrogant officials have feelings too!

THURSDAY, 3rd. Today brings a solar eclipse in your solar house of group activities which may make you uncomfortably aware of a gap in your life. Grab the chance to get out and about meeting folk who'll bring a breath of fresh air into your social scene.

FRIDAY, 4th. You're super-sensitive to the most subtle clues and hints that folk above you on the professional tree seem to be directing your way, but before you act on your insights you should wait to check things out a little more thoroughly. You're in a gullible mental state and tend to believe the best of everyone despite all evidence to the contrary. I don't say that they're deliberately out to lure you into trouble, but I wouldn't rule out the possibility entirely. A tricky and treacherous day.

SATURDAY, 5th. Once you come to a decision about your intuitive insights you're not one to shilly-shally around wondering what to do next. That's obvious on this Guy Fawkes' Day when you take direct action to quell a rumour, set the record straight or find out precisely what your partner's really thinking. Instinctively you know when you need to attack falsehoods at their source, so trust to a hunch concerning your intimate economic, inheritance or erotic affairs. Today's fiery stars show the promise of starting up a blaze all of your own!

SUNDAY, 6th. A super-sensitive mood persists today, but once the pressure for you to follow someone else's lead is removed you'll feel much more able to communicate your own insights and intuitions. A hunch could lead to professional progress, but don't be too shy to let anyone know what you're thinking, as they're likely to take you much more seriously than you expect. You fear mockery, but will encounter understanding.

MONDAY, 7th. Capricorns are normally very good at organisation, and today that's an underestatement! When fortunate Jupiter beams helpful rays at the highly original planet Uranus, some stunning insights are on their way. Of course inspiration alone isn't enough to get the ball rolling but you can rest assured that you've got the practical wherewithal to put your ideas into practice. This should be a lucky and progressive time!

TUESDAY, 8th. The fortunate vibes continue today with a generous and benevolent atmosphere surrounding you in all you do. A wealthy or well-heeled friend might give a welcoming hand. Perhaps someone who believes in you and your talents will provide the impetus to make some of your stunning ideas come to fruition.

WEDNESDAY, 9th. At last there's a little light at the end of the tunnel as Saturn's obstructive influence relents and begins to melt the ice around certain blocked and suspended situations. Ponderously at first, but then picking up pace, your mind begins to work once more with your accustomed ease and fluency. Communication lines that were apparently cut off for good may begin to heal, helping to break down the sense of isolation you've had recently.

THURSDAY, 10th. As ever-youthful Mercury skips into your solar house of future hopes and wishes, so you're catapulted into a busy and bustling span when your creative cranium will overflow with bright ideas and inventive innovations. Think in terms of your long-term perspectives.

FRIDAY, 11th. If you seriously hope to achieve the egalitarian and idealistic world of your dreams, sooner or later you'll have to discuss the practical steps you intend to take. Seize the opportunity of Friday's supremely sensible stars to discuss pragmatic problems with your friends, acquaintances and fellow idealists. If you're prepared to work as a team you'll be surprised at how many positive and constructive suggestions you can come up with between you. You're not likely to achieve overnight miracles, but the slow but sure path is the one that promises success.

SATURDAY, 12th. It's not often that canny Capricorns are persuaded to part with cash by a glib acquaintance but Saturday's spontaneous stars put you in an impulsive and spendthrift frame of mind. You usually know the value of money, so don't spoil your carefully created reputation as the saver of the zodiac by splashing out like there's no tomorrow!

SUNDAY, 13th. As the most charming, charismatic and eloquent member of your social circle, you'll be chosen to represent your pals in any public meetings that require an expressive spokesperson. Don't let your natural reserve hold you back, for you really are the best person for the job. You're divinely diplomatic now, so use your persuasive powers to dissolve any cliques that are forming amongst your friends and restore a sense of harmony and unity.

MONDAY, 14th. You're all set to be the star turn in your social circle today as your friends and associates acknowledge the value of your personal contribution to a group effort. Don't let your natural reticence hold you back from accepting their praise, for you're in a powerful position to set an enlightened and ethical example to any less principled people.

TUESDAY, 15th. Mini Mercury is caught in Saturn's firm grip and organised in a methodical manner that'll have you thinking in terms of lists and rotas for the rest of the day. While your mind's blessed with such a sensible grasp of the practicalities of life, you'd be wise to deal with the details of your future plans, as it's careful and conscientious planning that will make all the difference between success and failure.

WEDNESDAY, 16th. If some of the more radical notions you've encountered in the last few months have seemed just too ruthless and drastic to really take seriously, you'll be pleased to discover that there are other ways to bring this world of ours up to date without the violent overthrow of all traditions. A constructive approach that promises change without revolution is what you're seeking, and a new friend could have just the answer. Political discussions yield interesting results.

THURSDAY, 17th. The fine arts have an almost magnetic attraction for you these days. Poetry, painting, opera and ballet will all allow you to discover fresh funds of personal sensitivity as you find genuine pleasures in the creative achievements of others. You can shut out the mundane world with ease and lovingly lose yourself in the magic of heroes and heroines, soaring crescendos and moving melodies. You're a very suave, civilised and sophisticated wee Goat today!

FRIDAY, 18th. The Spanish Inquisition's got nothing on you today as you can root out any hidden or inhibiting emotional hang-ups that have been ruining your rapport with children. A creative venture needs your concentrated attention, for by pruning away aspects and activities that have become outdated or redundant, you'll make way for a fresh initiative.

SATURDAY, 19th. Those born under your sign are prone to occasional feelings of despondency and depression. With Mother Moon in the cold grasp of your ruling planet Saturn, it's too easy to feel low, miserable and inferior now. Pull yourself together, Capricorn, for you've got a lot going for you. There's no sense at all in feeling that you are being put upon and generally ground down. Count your blessings – you pride yourself on being realistic, so give yourself some credit for your achievements and prospects!

SUNDAY, 20th. Powerful passions in one form or another are sure to result from the astral encounter between the

Sun and Pluto in your solar house of future hopes. A profound transformation in all that you thought desirable is taking place as you dig deeply inside yourself to discover just which future path is the one for you. You must eliminate hopes that are no longer appropriate to your own path or live to regret it.

MONDAY, 21st. If you've really put your foot in it with your partner in life lately, whatever you do don't try to make amends now – for you're liable to rub salt in the wound merely by opening the subject up once more. I know you're sorry, but just saying so won't help matters. Let your peevish, petulant and pouting partner sleep on it for a while longer before you make your move.

TUESDAY, 22nd. With the winter solstice now only a month away, it's time to join the flora and fauna in their annual hibernation. Settle back into retirement and go about your business in a quiet and private way. You're just not interested in doing anything too public and are quite happy to reflect and reminisce upon your past as well as your future.

WEDNESDAY, 23rd. There are some chums who are very dear to you but somehow, what with one thing and another, you haven't seen them for ages. Now's your chance to make contact once more and renew the bonds of affection. If no one fits the bill maybe it's time you stepped out a bit more in your social circle and formed a few closer attachments? There are some mighty lovable lads and lassies around if you take the trouble to look!

THURSDAY, 24th. Intimate affairs move you deeply as you tune in to deeper emotions and realise just how strong and powerful your feelings are. Your most treasured possessions are imbued with a charm and magic that holds so many memories of childhood happiness, so why not rummage through your drawers or your attic and take a sentimental stroll down Memory Lane? If others lay claim to the same possessions, don't dispute, as your memories are your own and can never be taken away.

FRIDAY, 25th. You'll be in great demand amongst your more spiritually minded pals this Friday as you demonstrate the depth and delicacy of your intuitive appreciation of abstract feelings. Anything from a lively discussion to a helping hand to those in distress will appeal to your better nature now, and give you a chance to shine. Your responsible attitude earns the respect of all around you.

SATURDAY, 26th. As you ponder on the many possibilities that could lie open to you in the future, a sudden brainwave coming like a bolt from the blue will set you thinking on a different track altogether. Your pals will be delighted to see you taking a detour into territory that could prove packed with fun and opportunity. Lateral thinking is the key now, so let your thoughts wander at will.

SUNDAY, 27th. Normally you're quite clear about precisely where your own limitations lie, but under Sunday's intellectually expansive sky you have an excellent chance to question your personal boundaries and beliefs. Perhaps there are some subjects you've always shunned that would prove fruitful and fascinating to you now? Spiritualist, supernatural and psychological studies interest you, so why not investigate a little more closely?

MONDAY, 28th. There's no point in trying to beat 'em, and in your case it may be better to join 'em! Your method of communication is very harsh and in fact you can be a real tyrant this moody Monday. You will have your own battles with bureaucracy to contend with, so don't start leaning on others.

TUESDAY, 29th. Don't let a fervent and fanatical friend put you off with their dogmatic attitude, even if they have a point that's worth pursuing. Sort out the priorities of a shared venture with any folk involved, as only by ruthlessly pruning unnecessary or misleading ideas from your plans can you proceed properly on to the next phase. Cut through confusion at a stroke.

WEDNESDAY, 30th. If you're interested in superstitions or folklore, Mercury's initiation into your twelfth house of mystery will open up your mind even more to things that go bump in the night and all that's unknown. From the outside you appear to have clammed up, but your inner world is buzzing with inspirational ideas, intriguing thoughts and delicious daydreams.

DECEMBER

THURSDAY, 1st. For a down-to-earth wee Goat you've a sensational supply of sympathetic spiritual understanding, and that's what your friends and associates will appreciate most now. Give them the benevolent benefit of your experience over any issue connected with a cause you're all devoted to, for with your sagacious wisdom and their devout dedication you can hardly fail to achieve your shared aspirations!

FRIDAY, 2nd. There's a psychic and super-sensitive feel to Friday which makes you much more moody and prickly than usual. The reason for this is that you're tuning into mystical higher forces that imbue you with a greater awareness of your deepest, innermost feelings. An emotional corner will be turned that'll help you look forward to a calm and contented future, so don't hang back out of reluctance or timidity.

SATURDAY, 3rd. Tuckered out is hardly an adequate phrase to describe your state this Saturday, as you've given your all to make sure that everything comes up to your sensational standards and now you deserve a day of total peace and quiet to recuperate. Pull up your favourite armchair, pick out your favourite films from the array on offer, and immerse yourself in a quiet pool of pure pleasure!

SUNDAY, 4th. The planetary picture isn't very bright at the moment, so don't look for a sudden break in the clouds. If anything you're feeling even less sanguine about your chances, owing to negative news and depressing rumours. It's very difficult for you to find a constructive solution to your problems whilst your mood remains so melancholy, so postpone all important meetings and talks if at all possible. Local journeys all seem to take longer than usual for one reason or another.

MONDAY, 5th. A backlash could cause you financial fright, due either to forgetfulness or your tendency to sweep some things under the carpet. You've got to weigh up your incomings and outgoings now, otherwise you'll be permanently out of pocket. Immoral earnings or plundered booty could cause problems too. Romantically you're ardent and passionate!

TUESDAY, 6th. While Venus lingers in your house of future hopes you should exert your charms and forge friendly links with pals and acquaintances who are in tune with your aspirations. You need to know that you're held in affectionate esteem by your friends, and will be ready to go out of your way to demonstrate just how likeable and lovable you really are. You're such a social charmer, Capricorn!

WEDNESDAY, 7th. You may overhear a conversation or pick up some hints from something someone says that will put you on the track of a savings scheme or method of accounting that could solve your problems. Discreet enquiries will fill you in on the details, and once you know the ins and outs you should again listen to the inclination of your intuition. You're sensitive to subtle clues now.

THURSDAY, 8th. For such a dutiful and sober person it's really hard to see how today's stars could possibly make you more methodical, sensible and capable than you are already, but when the financially fortunate rays of velvet Venus beam good luck at your ruling planet, Saturn, you have the chance to turn your normal thrifty traits into monetary profit. If you act on the impulses that today's astral array provides, you can be sure of a profitable start to the upcoming New Year.

FRIDAY, 9th. Has the spiritual side of life been neglected amidst the practical pressures of your world? Well, from today you should devote much more time and attention to an ever-expanding awareness of the religious, spiritual or occult assumptions underlying your existence, for the light of genial Jupiter illuminates the most secret recesses of your mind, and you have a whole year to deepen your understanding, aided by the sympathetic stars. Your own ego must take a back seat whilst you tune in to the true meaning of life, the universe and everything!

SATURDAY, 10th. Futuristic trends are so exciting now, and some of your more outspoken pals so inspiring, that you're ready to throw in your lot with anyone preaching radical revolution! If you're very much aware of your motives and know in advance how much time, effort and money you're willing to put into a particular venture, you could succeed beyond your wildest dreams. The least hint of reckless over-kill, however, and you'll be stranded out on a limb, far from all support. Proceed with just a little extra caution.

SUNDAY, 11th. There's a secretive smile playing on your luscious lips as you keep people guessing about just what's put you in such a good mood. It's a gentle game you're playing to maintain your mysterious and enigmatic image, but it could be something as simple as a quiet word of support from someone you respect, or news that aid you've offered in private has had the desired effect, that's making you so content. Let folk build more elaborate explanations if it keeps them happy!

MONDAY, 12th. You'll find that you want to direct most of your energies into getting out of the traps that life has laid for you recently. You will be spurred on to greater things intellectually, but you'll also favour getting away from any restricting situation that hampers your vision. Expansion and growth are hellishly important to you now.

TUESDAY, 13th. You've done your share of socialising, and now's your chance to withdraw from the hubbub of the world in order to reflect in peace on your spiritual state. Think deeply about the true meaning of this festive season – whatever your personal beliefs, you're keen to dwell on the ideals of peace on earth and goodwill to all. Maybe there's something you can do to promote your principles, such as visiting someone who's poorly?

WEDNESDAY, 14th. Self-indulgent starlight saps your strength and undermines all your good intentions until you can hardly be bothered to do a thing if it's not directly related to satisfying your senses in some way. Consequently you're admirably suited to an evening's undemanding entertainment with hedonistic pals – or perhaps a few hours stretched out on your softest sofa, with loved ones waiting on your every whim, appeals? Well, you're free to dream of all manner of delights!

THURSDAY, 15th. Party time! You're such a businesslike soul that that may not sound like good news, but once you get your glad rags on and grab the hand of your beloved, you'll welcome today's opportunity to let your hair down. In fact the spirit of amour will motivate you Thursday if it's given half a chance, so make the first loving move and let the wine, music and starshine take care of the rest! A kindly gesture from a youngster will touch you deeply. After all, Christmas is just around the corner.

FRIDAY, 16th. Healthwise this is a tricky time, with coughs and colds doing the rounds, so don't go getting into glamorous unseasonal clobber unless you're sure you're not going to catch a chill. Friday's stars also give a superbly sympathetic glow that makes you want to do all you can to aid the less fortunate of this world. That's all very admirable, but you won't help anyone if you give so much away that you're left impoverished yourself. Don't be a martyr, Capricorn – it's well known that under that crusty exterior there beats a heart of solid gold. You don't have to prove yourself all the time!

SATURDAY, 17th. A workmate may be smarting a bit because of the harsh words you had to say about their unfriendly attitude and malicious behaviour, and now you're suffering the painful pangs of guilt as a result. Don't be so hard on yourself, for the chances are that they deserved all that they got, and more besides! Nervous tension may make you feel under the weather, so pamper yourself a little.

SUNDAY, 18th. Sunday's seasonal Full Moon gives you another chance to reassess your employment position – is it time you moved on to a more fulfilling post? Or should you press for more congenial conditions? Don't shy away from awkward conclusions to your searching questions. Healthwise you must also rid yourself of habits that aren't doing you any good at all.

MONDAY, 19th. Astute, shrewd and calculating are three little words that describe you to a T this Monday, when you're at your practical best. All of these qualities are pronounced in the weeks ahead as clever Mercury moves into your Sun sign. I'll make no bones about it – he'll be working very well, wheeling and dealing, plotting and planning, and organising a takeover of your ambitious realms.

TUESDAY, 20th. If you're called on to explain your beliefs to a crowd of friends or even certain critics, you needn't fear stage fright under such outspoken and certain stars. You know perfectly well what you want to say to anyone arguing the opposite view, and with your cogent and confident arguments you're sure to win the day. A splendid day to consider long-term plans and outline a purpose that's both bold and soundly reasoned.

WEDNESDAY, 21st. There is a desire within for you to sort out the many inner turbulences you have felt over the past months. You are undergoing a spiritual metamorphosis, and because of this your wants and needs are changing. Today brings a brighter outlook, but don't stand back and do nothing when this is a time to be curious about life.

THURSDAY, 22nd. The majestic Sun sits lavishly in your very own sign as the winter solstice dawns, awakening you from your emotional slumbers. Your self-confidence is richly renewed and any shadowy feelings of inferiority are chased cheerfully away, forecasting better and more bountiful days to come. Your perfectly poochy personality is a shining light to us all in these dark days of winter.

FRIDAY, 23rd. That impulsive and reckless mood is still making you as jumpy as a cat on a hot tin roof, and today you won't take no for an answer as you try to explain your new theories to all and sundry, whether they want to listen or not! Don't take offence if folk don't seem as excited as you about your ideas – it's probably not meant personally, and they may just have something else, such as Christmas, on their minds.

SATURDAY, 24th. Your eyes light up at the prospect of brilliant Yuletide excitement, merry parties and gorgeous gifts, but before you don your overcoat and prepare to enjoy the festive fun there are certain practical matters that must be attended to. In fact, you're an organisational whizz today, able to produce a consistent and constructive plan of action without batting an eyelid. Get your chores done and the final shopping in and you'll enjoy the dazzling Christmas Eve atmosphere all the more.

SUNDAY, 25th. Merry Christmas, Capricorn! No matter how comfy and convenient your domestic celebrations are, tales you've heard tell of Yuletide extravaganzas overseas or in the homes of the rich and famous have inspired you with some very immoderate and excessive ideas. You want to do well by your family, and put on a fabulous feast, and there's nothing wrong with that, so why am I concerned? It's the thorny subject of money that's on my mind, and

186

quite honestly it should be on yours as well. I hope that you've kept within your budget, for I'll bet most folk would prefer a more traditional celebration this year.

MONDAY, 26th. Your confidence for external affairs returns with today's super-charged stars. You're ready to do battle on behalf of your beliefs, whatever the odds, and that's just the kind of aggressive attitude that will put your opponents to flight. You also have the honourable integrity to hold back from rubbing their nose in any defeat, and that will earn you more admiration than anything else. Don't wait for overseas contacts or long-distance pals to contact you – if you take the initiative and dial the number you can make this a Boxing Day to remember.

TUESDAY, 27th. Those Goats who are back to work today will be swept along on a tide of socialising, while jobless souls will be wise to keep their eyes open for unexpected opportunities to get their foot in the door of employment. Parties and sudden chances to progress are all very well, but you can't help being unsettled by the upheaval in the steady routine you're accustomed to. Don't let it all throw you off your stride and you'll be fine.

WEDNESDAY, 28th. If your social life is already flourishing, you can look forward to a busy and bustling day spent visiting, phoning or chatting to your pals. If you're in need of a firm friend, now's the time to start putting out feelers and making new acquaintances. Just passing the time of day with someone congenial will cheer you up no end.

THURSDAY, 29th. At heart you're an intensely emotional soul, but no one would suspect it Thursday as you bustle about issuing instructions and generally displaying a genius

187

for organisation. Write down your ideas in a methodical and systematic way, especially regarding your professional aims and ambitions, as any plans you devise now will be rational, realistic and reasonable.

FRIDAY, 30th. A Friday when the women around you are the epitome of radiance and reassurance. If there's someone in your life who has stood by you through thick and thin, or just been there when you needed them, now's the time to show your appreciation and let them know they're the only one in the world for you. Organise a night out or a gift in their honour and you'll be feeling just as thrilled as they are!

SATURDAY, 31st. The Moon in your Sun sign make a dramatic trine to Mars on this last day of the year, bringing out self-assertive characteristics that will put you on the road to both mental and spiritual fulfilment. Let your mind think openly and don't hold back any thoughts that could be useful in the upcoming annum. Be a positive and optimistic soul, Capricorn. Happy Hogmanay!